THE WORLD PEACE WAY

Six Keys to Health and Harmony for All

DR. WILL TUTTLE

Karuna • Middletown, CA

The World Peace Way:
Six Keys to Health and Harmony for All

Karuna
Middletown, CA
www.WorldPeaceDiet.com

Cover art and inside art by Madeleine Tuttle

ISBN: 979-8-9902104-4-8
Library of Congress Control Number: 2024919188

Disclaimer:
The ideas and suggestions in this book are intended for educational purposes only. The information provided in this book is for personal and spiritual development. It does not constitute medical advice. This book is not intended to replace medical advice, or to diagnose, prescribe or treat any disease, condition or injury.

THE WORLD PEACE WAY

*Six Keys to Health and
Harmony for All*

Dr. Will Tuttle

TABLE OF CONTENTS

PREFACE

"Words are also seeds, and when dropped into the invisible spiritual substance, they grow and bring forth after their kind."
—CHARLES FILLMORE

"We must recognize that our emotions and thoughts can manifest physically in our bodies."
—JOHN SARNO, M.D.

The Good News

The World Peace Way, companion volume to our recently-published book, *Food for Freedom*, is intended to provide practical ideas and suggestions to support all of us in our essential efforts to reclaim our health and to rescue our world. *The World Peace Way* also serves as a companion to our earlier book, *The World Peace Diet*. The six keys discussed in *The World Peace Way*—nutrition, spiritual practice, relationships, movement, nature, and creativity—can open doorways that help us to thrive in our daily lives, and to more fully embody the ideas in both *Food for Freedom* and *The World Peace Diet*.

The basic good news in these books is that we are all generously provided with physical bodies that require no animals to be harmed to acquire the nutrients necessary to celebrate our lives on every level. Further essential good news is that we, like all living beings, are not mere material objects as our culture's pseudo-religion, scientism, proclaims. Rather, our physical bodies are transitory manifestations of our true nature as fundamentally non-physical and eternal consciousness. We are spiritual beings and everything about our earthly life is profoundly affected by the nature of our attitudes, awareness, and actions. As we become more conscious about the quality of our thoughts, feelings, and intentions, as well as of our food, lifestyle choices, relationships, and ways of moving, creating, and being, we can dramatically improve not only our physical and psychological health, but also increase our contribution to the overall well-being of our society as a whole. This book provides a broad range of tools we can proactively employ in service to the understanding we are building, and to the life we are creating.

While *Food for Freedom* and *The World Peace Diet* are primarily focused on providing more in-depth and inspiring understanding of the "why"—why it is liberating to question mainstream cultural narratives about food and health—*The World Peace Way* focuses on the "how." It aims to provide a host of practical ways through which we can proactively bring our lives into congruence with our aspirations, and more fully embody the freedom, vitality, and joy that we would like to see gracing all living beings. This book is in many ways a workbook, with a variety of practices, techniques, and suggestions that many people have found to be helpful over decades, centuries, and millennia. Our individual adventure is to discover and engage whatever tools and resources resonate most significantly with us.

Virtually all of us intuitively understand that world peace is based on inner peace. If we could miraculously transform our society into one of abundance, equality, compassion, freedom, and harmony, it would quickly degenerate into injustice and conflict unless all of us as individuals could maintain the necessary level of enlightened consciousness required to ensure this degree of peacefulness in our shared social reality. We are currently failing in this because we have been indoctrinated from infancy into long-established norms and cultural narratives that hijack us away from our inherent capacity to embody the wisdom, harmony, and compassion that characterize our true nature.

Collectively and individually, our life experience reflects the vibratory level of our awareness, and by making the effort to free ourselves from counterproductive conditioning, we can become a force for raising awareness and inspiring others. In many ways, our Earth seems to be a school designed to help train us to develop our inner resources, and through this process, to peel off the veils of delusion, and connect more deeply with our noumenal essence rather than mistakenly identify with the shallow mask of our phenomenal selfhood. With diligence, we can discover the many ways through which the outer world mirrors the inner, and how we unavoidably experience the fruits of our thoughts, beliefs, and actions.

The Way and Its Power

The World Peace Way: this word "way" has many overtones of meaning, including path, journey, process, and road, but also carries a sense of revealing a universal set of principles based on ancient wisdom teachings. Christians are known to refer to their teachings as The Way, and the pivotal Chinese word Tao is also traditionally translated as the Way, as is the Buddhist term *dharmata*, conveying an understanding and way of living that brings our minds and hearts into harmony with the larger cosmic forces, and confers freedom, health, and wisdom. When we find our way, we reconnect with the authentic truth of our being, and this universal reconnection guides us in the daily particulars of our lives.

The World Peace Way is based on universal principles that have been articulated in the world's wisdom traditions for centuries:

- the Golden Rule;
- reciprocity and causality;
- the reality of spiritual healing;
- the oneness of mind and body;
- the primacy of consciousness over matter;
- the interconnectedness of all expressions of life;
- the healing power of love and understanding;
- the inherent presence of our most valuable ally, our inner guidance system;
- the importance of questioning, and freeing ourselves from, social conditioning;
- and the transcendent unity of the Source of all life amid its diverse expressions.

From these universal principles, which cannot be completely captured as mere verbal concepts, we can intuit The World Peace Way: inner and outer practices and ways of being that support health on every level and that bring us into harmony with our true nature.

One of the main teachings underlying the ideas in this book is the remarkable value of being willing not only to learn but to unlearn. We have all been wounded by schooling systems that are designed and structured to instill conformity, obedience to outside authority, and a shallow self-concept based on materialism, consumerism, and fitting in. We have a lot to unlearn.

We've also been deliberately harmed by deceptive media, governmental, societal, and medical narratives that are both parasitic and predatory, and by an ever-increasing profusion of actual poisons that assault us through processed and contaminated foods and beverages, air, and water, as well as through pharmaceuticals, electromagnetic fields, and weather warfare technologies, among other things.

It is essential to proactively question official narratives about practically everything, and to diligently examine and comprehend the agenda of plutocratic globalist forces. They operate through media channels, education, business, and virtually all governance, from the United Nations, the World Health Organization, the World Economic Forum, and the Bank of International Settlements, to national, state, and local governments and agencies throughout the world, which are inescapably and relentlessly pressured to do their bidding.

Our Inner Guidance System

Our greatest ally in this healthy discernment is our inner guidance system. As we awaken out of the trance of materialism that has been inflicted on us by being raised in cultural institutions that reflect ten thousand years of animal agriculture, we can make the essential effort to unlearn the harmful assumptions that pervade our society, and to cultivate a holistic understanding of the oneness of our body-mind as a manifestation of our non-corporeal true nature. As one example, Dr. John Sarno, MD, has discovered and demonstrated throughout an extensive career in medical practice that a remarkably large proportion of our chronic pains and ailments are due to what he refers to as TMS: The Mind-body Syndrome.[1] He has been exceptionally successful in helping people to heal by introducing them to the idea that unconscious and un-faced emotional stress is a primary cause of tension in the body, and that this tension manifests as a wide variety of pains, disorders, and medical conditions. These maladies not only generate enormous suffering, but also massive profits to a medical industry that is trained to ignore the mind-body connection and to focus on providing material fixes for what are often lifestyle, emotional, and spiritual problems.[2]

There are many more examples of successful treatment of illness through mental and spiritual approaches from ancient times to the present day as I discuss in Chapter Eight of *Food for Freedom*. The essential point is that we have large and little-understood capacities for maintaining radiant vibrancy and health, and that these capacities are fully available to us as part of our heritage as essentially spiritual beings. The key is to combine the practical lifestyle tools in this book, both outer and inner, with the underlying positive approach of mobilizing our intuitive wisdom, questioning our conditioning, and rescuing ourselves from the internalized cultural program that reduces us to mere material objects.

One life lives through us all, and we are that life itself. Exploring, cultivating, and engaging these ideas, we are treading The World Peace Way.

Welcome, and enjoy the beckoning journey!

Chapter One

THE FIRST KEY: HEALTHY DIET

"Our food should be our medicine and our medicine our food."
—HIPPOCRATES

"Science itself may have become a threat to overall population health."
—JOHN IOANNIDIS, M.D.

"Gardening is perhaps the greatest act of love and reverence we could give to the Earth, ourselves, our families and communities."
—ZACH BUSH, M.D.

Plant-sourced Foods for Freedom

The first key to healthy living—healthy diet—refers to food primarily, but also to water, air, and personal care products, and further, it can include what we feed our mind through our reading, entertainment, music, media, conversations, and so forth. Our word diet derives from the Greek word *diaita*, meaning "way of life," and it is in this broader sense that we are using the word diet here.

Regarding food as our edible sustenance, it is foundational to eat a completely plant-sourced (vegan) diet for optimal health and awareness. Animal-sourced foods concentrate three types of harmful toxins: cumulative, inherent, and metaphysical. Cumulative toxins are the residues from chemical fertilizers, pesticides, fungicides, herbicides, and other environmental toxins such as heavy metals, PCBs, dioxin, nuclear radiation, and other noxious substances, all of which concentrate in the tissues, mammary secretions, and eggs of animals. Glyphosate, atrazine, paraquat, neonicotinoids, and hundreds more carcinogenic, endocrine-disruptive, and neurotoxic chemicals are sprayed on crops that are fed to animals.

Our human-generated poisons eventually end up in the waters of oceans, rivers and lakes. Cows, pigs, chickens, and turkeys are routinely fed fish meal, to boost weight-gain and milk and egg output, which comes either from wild-caught fish or factory-farmed fish, both of which concentrate chemical and heavy metal toxins in their flesh hundreds of thousands or millions of times more than the water in which they live. This is because they constantly pass water over their gills to extract oxygen, as well as water contaminants, and they are additionally at the upper ends of long food chains that concentrate toxins all the way up. Consequently, eating marine animals, or animals whose feed is "enriched" with fish meal, significantly increases our risk of cancer and other highly profitable chronic diseases.[3] It is ironic that many of us, in a misguided effort to clean up our diets, forsake so-called meat and "just" eat fish, dairy and eggs, which are probably the three most harmful foods in terms of concentrated toxicity.

Besides these thousands of different environmental toxins, animal-sourced foods also concentrate the ten thousand different vaccines, medications, and other pharmaceuticals that have been approved to be routinely injected into farmed animals or mixed into their feed, or forced into them through baths and sprays. About 70 percent of manufactured antibiotics are administered to farmed animals to boost weight gain and facilitate short-term survival in their toxic environments,[4] as well as many different types of artificial hormones and other drugs and chemicals to increase profitability, including devastatingly harmful biotech modified RNA vaccines.[5] So-called organic meat, dairy products, and eggs will likely contain a lower concentration of these toxins because these operators are mandated to refrain from using non-organic feeds and pharmaceuticals, but the animals are still eating, drinking, and breathing, and the broad range of environmental toxins in the soil, water, and air will inevitably concentrate in their flesh and secretions.

The second type of toxins are inherent. Animal-sourced foods contain large and complex proteins that acidify our blood and tissues when we metabolize them, as well as saturated fat and cholesterol that, in excess, are linked with diabetes, obesity, liver disease, heart disease, atherosclerosis, and other chronic conditions. It cannot be overemphasized that, as has been acknowledged even by the mainstream U.S. Academy of Nutrition and Dietetics,[6] all the nutrients needed for thriving at all stages of life (infancy, childhood, adulthood, pregnancy, lactation, athletics, and elder years) are provided by plants. Aided by the alchemical wizardry of photosynthesis, plants synthesize and provide all the nutrients we need to be healthy, including carbohydrates, proteins, fats, vitamins, minerals, and fiber.

Complex carbohydrates and starches are plentiful in plants, and are the basic, clean-burning fuel that we metabolize to power our muscles, brain, and organs. As the word carbohydrate implies, they are composed of just three basic elements, carbon, hydrogen, and oxygen, and burn cleanly to glucose for energy, with easily eliminated carbon dioxide and water as waste products. Plants are also able, with the help of bacteria, to fix atmospheric nitrogen and thus to create all of the amino acids that we use to create the many hundreds of thousands of different proteins that build and repair tissues and facilitate bodily processes. Plants create all the fatty acids and lipids that are essential to healthy living, as well as providing the fiber that is indispensable to maintaining a robust microbiome for efficient digestion. Additionally, they extract all the needed minerals from the soil, and create the so-called vitamins required as well, with the possible exception of vitamin D, which is a hormone that we synthesize through exposure to sunlight, and which is also present in some fungal foods such as mushrooms, and B12, which is synthesized by bacteria, and is also present in some plant foods such as mushrooms, nori, kimchi, and tempeh.[7]

Though there are carnivorous and omnivorous animals, most are designed, like us, to eat plants and get nutrients directly from plants. Our physiology is decidedly herbivorous, as discussed in *The World Peace Diet*[8] and as has been clearly established by nutritional research,[9] as well as by the example of millions of people thriving on completely plant-sourced diets. Instead of obtaining necessary fats, proteins, and minerals from the flesh and secretions of animals, our bodies can obtain all needed nutrients directly from plants. By cutting out the "middle animal," we drastically reduce the toxin load of our diet, and ensure the plentiful uptake of two essential nutrients, complex carbohydrates and fiber, which are non-existent in animal-sourced foods. Complex carbohydrates are our basic human fuel, and fiber is essential to building a robust microbiome community of bacteria in our gut, and to healthy digestion and elimination.

In order to synthesize the amino acids that make up proteins, plants incorporate nitrogen into their foundational elements of carbon, oxygen, and hydrogen, and when we metabolize protein, especially animal protein, an acidic ash is created that our body must eliminate. It is well understood that a diet of excess protein causes inflammation, acidification of blood and tissues, and contributes to cancer, kidney disease, osteoporosis, arthritis, and other degenerative diseases. Because most people in industrialized countries eat diets high in animal-based foods, the hospitals are filled with people afflicted with diseases caused by excess acid and protein, as T. Colin Campbell and many other nutrition researchers have been explaining for years.[10]

Plant-sourced foods not only contain the vital carbohydrates, phytonutrients, and fiber essential to healthy living,[11] they typically have higher quality proteins than those in animal foods, reducing the risk of chronic disease.[12] When we eat proteins, whether from plants or animals, our bodies break them down to their constituent amino acids and then build the needed proteins from these amino acids. Because plant proteins tend to be relatively simple and easy to metabolize, and because animal proteins (found in muscles, milk, and eggs) tend to be much larger, more complex, and unwieldy, more energy is needed to break down and recombine animal proteins, and these also create a significantly higher acid load.[13] As the documentary film *The Game Changers*[14] demonstrates, many elite athletes are realizing this, and finding that transitioning to completely plant-sourced foods provides them with more energy, endurance, and strength, and dramatically reduces recovery time in training.[15]

There are no carbohydrates in meat, eggs, and most dairy products; they are primarily protein and fat. Protein cannot be stored in the body, but must be metabolized, leading to acidification and inflammation, whereas fat is easily stored, leading to being overweight and obese, which now afflicts two-thirds of the U.S. population.[16] The complex carbohydrates and starches that are plentiful in whole plant-sourced foods are easily converted to glucose, the main fuel for our muscles, organs, and brain. Our brain, for example, though only two percent of our body weight, requires twenty percent of our energy[17] in the form of glucose. The complex carbohydrates found in fruits, vegetables, whole grains, beans, potatoes, squashes, and other plant-sourced foods are the cleanest and most efficient source of glucose, not just for healthy brain function, but as fuel for our muscles and other bodily processes.[18] Our digestive and circulatory systems are not equipped to process high amounts of fat and protein,[19] which clog, acidify, and harm our blood, arteries, and intestines, leading to higher risk for heart disease, strokes, atherosclerosis, and diabetes, as well as breast, prostrate, and colon cancer, among other conditions.

Other inherently harmful constituents of animal-sourced foods include saturated fats, trans-fats, and cholesterol, all of which contribute to arterial damage, heart disease, strokes, diabetes, arthritis, cancers, and other problems.[20] There is also the lactose in dairy products, for which about 75% of us (mainly non-Europeans and non-Indians) have not evolved a tolerance, and thus cannot digest without upsetting our digestive system.[21] Additionally, one widely-consumed protein, casein, the main protein in bovine milk, is particularly toxic for us humans.[22] This is because we lack the enzyme rennin, which calves naturally have, to break it down.[23] Casein is an especially large and unwieldy protein, which is concentrated in cheese, skim milk, and yogurt. Widespread human consumption of cow's milk and its bovine casein provides an ongoing bonanza for the medical-pharmaceutical complex, providing a reliable flood of sore throats, runny noses, ear aches, sinusitis, eczema, allergies, inflammation, osteoporosis, digestive issues, diabetes, and cardiovascular disease, as well as breast, prostate, and colon cancer, among other conditions.[24] There are further harmful substances in animal-sourced foods, such as the carcinogenic heterocyclic amines that form when animal flesh is cooked.[25] We can get all the nutrients we need to thrive directly from plants. When we pass plants through animals, we lose essential nutrients such as carbohydrates and fiber, degrade the proteins and essential fatty acids, and add environmental toxins, as well as substances we are not designed to handle, such as trans fats, cholesterol, and casein.

The idea that plant-sourced foods can be poisonous or harmful has been proclaimed by some animal food advocates, and while it is of course true that some plants such as certain mushrooms are toxic to us humans, and that some uncooked legumes such as kidney beans contain lectins that can make us sick, the fact is that we simply don't eat those rare poisonous plants and no one considers eating uncooked kidney beans. Additionally, when there are cases of harmful bacteria in produce, for example salmonella found in lettuce, the source of the harmful bacteria is typically irrigation water that has been contaminated by animal agricultural runoff.

While some people may have sensitivities to certain plant-sourced foods, it is clear that the great civilizations that historically supported large and thriving human populations did so on the calorie-dense staples of rice, wheat, corn, millet, barley, rye, beans, potatoes, squashes, and other plant-sourced high-starch foods. Healthy fruits, nuts, seeds, vegetables, tubers, berries, legumes, and mushrooms have historically provided additional nutrition. Madeleine and I have been thriving for over forty years on a completely plant-sourced way of eating, and there are millions of healthy long-term vegans who, like us, demonstrate these truths.

We are born into a beautiful and benevolent planet that can easily supply all the nutrients required to thrive without forcing us to abandon our compassion and harden our hearts, and stab, exploit, and abuse animals in order to be healthy. We are not born into a satanic planet requiring us to be merciless killers, but we *are* raised within a deluded socio-cultural food orientation that is based on the demonic practice of guiltlessly and relentlessly harming other sentient beings for our supposed benefit and pleasure.

The third type of toxin that concentrates in animal-sourced foods can be referred to as metaphysical toxins, discussed at length in Chapter Eight of *The World Peace Diet*. In brief, the animals we are eating are forced to endure both chronic and acute fear as well as chronic and acute pain due to their routine mutilation, forced impregnation, confinement, medication, exploitation, transportation, brutal beatings, complete inability to form natural relationships with their own kind, and eventual slaughter. This causes not just physical hormones like adrenalin to be excreted into the flesh and secretions of these animals, but also adrenochrome, as well as the reality of pain, terror, anxiety, fury, panic, depression, helplessness, and misery. These are realities, and we live in a culture that has become so disconnected from its basic intelligence and awareness by ten thousand years of animal exploitation and the resultant materialism that it has become almost completely blind and numb to these realities. Because scientism cannot quantify these realities, it assumes they do not exist.

Though we are taught to studiously ignore the fact that we are causing and eating hideous suffering, the reality is unavoidable. Inflicting anxiety and depression on millions of vulnerable animals, we eat their pain and misery, and find that anxiety and depression in humans drive the demand for medications contributing to the pharmaceutical industry's greatest profits. We can be sure these connections will never be discussed in the media, in medical schools, or in government agencies due to the impact of decades of pharmaceutical-medical profits and influence deriving from psychiatric medications. Consequently, the connection between our psychological abuse of animals and our own mental suffering never enters our minds, and is in fact, to most people, an uncomfortable and well-suppressed idea. For the medical industry, there is no money in healthy and happy people; these are the greatest threats to its power and profits.

The stark reality is that while slaughterhouses, stockyards, feedlots, and factory farms are among the most hellish, violent, abusive, ugly, and toxic places on this Earth, well-tended organic gardens, fields, and orchards are typically both beautiful and enjoyable to visit. Madeleine and I relish our time in our veganic food forest garden, not only appreciating the inherent beauty, fragrance, and harmony of the fruit and nut trees, the berry bushes and vines, and the herbs and vegetables growing, flourishing, and fruiting in their unique ways, but also tuning in to them to know which ones would like water, compost tea, trimming, and other care and nutrients. Animal agriculture is feeding on slavery, misery, betrayal, ugliness, and death; plant agriculture, when done mindfully and with care, is feeding on freedom, abundance, beauty, and life, benefitting not only the plants but also the larger community of living beings that a garden supports.

Organic and Unprocessed Foods

Another key to optimal nutrition is that our plant-sourced foods are also organic, whole and unprocessed, and as much as possible, locally grown. Organic has become more important than ever for three main reasons. First, commercial agriculture uses pesticides, herbicides, and chemical fertilizers that kill birds, fishes, and insects, and pollute and promote algae growth and dead zones in water, destroy the integrity of ecosystems, and harm the fungi and bacteria that make up the microbiome of the living soil. Organic agriculture strives to minimize pollution and harm to wildlife and ecosystems, and to build up the integrity of the soil microbiome in order to increase crop yields. Veganic agriculture, which additionally refrains from using any animal-sourced inputs such as bonemeal, bloodmeal, fishmeal, and manure, is even more clean and beneficial to local ecosystems.

Second, organic foods have far lower residues of pesticides and herbicides, which cause cancer, autoimmune diseases, liver disease, neurological problems, irritable bowel syndrome, and other conditions. For example, there are well-known links between the weedkiller paraquat and Parkinson's disease,[26] aluminum and Alzheimer's' disease,[27] mercury and neuro-degenerative disease,[28] and many more. Glyphosate, the main ingredient in Roundup (it's good to consider the deeper meaning of that word), is the most widely-used herbicide in the world, especially in the U.S., and is now so pervasive that it is virtually ubiquitous in all non-organic foods.[29] It is not only carcinogenic and neurotoxic,[30] but is also a broad-spectrum antibiotic, harming not only the microbiome of plants and of the soil, but also the microbiome in our digestive tract, leading to leaky gut, irritable bowel syndrome, and many other digestive issues.

For example, over the last twenty years or so, increasing numbers of people find they feel unwell when they eat wheat, and it's therefore increasingly fashionable to avoid wheat and to request gluten-free meals. What is hidden from public knowledge is that in the last twenty years, the commercial (non-organic) wheat industry has increasingly implemented the protocol of spraying wheat fields with glyphosate just prior to harvest, because glyphosate forces the plants into a violent death paroxysm in which all the wheat berries are released by the plants simultaneously, thereby increasing yield and profitability. Thus, non-organic wheat products are now virtually universally coated with glyphosate, a neurotoxic carcinogen that is also a broad-spectrum antibiotic that wreaks havoc with our gut flora. Ironically, it is "healthy" whole-wheat products that are most harmful when the wheat is non-organic because it is the outer bran layers that have the highest toxic residue levels.

Besides containing harmful residues of hundreds of other harmful agriculture chemicals, non-organic foods may be genetically-engineered. These so-called foods are known to be genetically unstable with a range of toxic effects, including allergenicity, carcinogenicity, suppression of the immune system, and nutrient depletion.[31] Though many of these GMO foods are primarily grown as livestock feed (corn, soy, alfalfa, cotton, and canola) they can also be found in consumer foods as well, and for this reason it is best to eat organic only, to minimize pesticide residues as well as genetically-engineered foods.[32] The pharmaceutical-chemical-agricultural complex is continually working to weaken organic standards, making it imperative to be vigilant in the face of emerging threats such as chemical coatings that may be sprayed over otherwise organic fruits and vegetables to increase shelf life.[33]

Third, organically grown plant-sourced foods are typically more nutritious than commercially grown versions because organic farmers, to be successful, tend to make an effort to build up the health of their soil so that their crops are naturally more resistant to disease and pests, because they do not rely on chemical fertilizers and pesticides. Healthier soil leads to more nutrients and minerals in the foods, and more life-force in the plants. For all these reasons, the best sources of foods are organic and veganic farms, orchards, and gardens. To be most assured of the quality of our foods, we can cultivate them ourselves, or get to know local farmers. We can grow sprouts continuously on our kitchen counter, and we can set up a sprouts and micro-greens growing table on our porch or balcony, along with tomatoes, peppers, zucchini, eggplants, and other vegetables in containers. With a little land, we can install raised beds and plant more vegetables, as well as herbs and berry bushes, and, if possible, some fruit and nut trees, and more.

For example, we have several neighbors who, like us, are tending small veganic food forests that include fruit and nut trees, raised beds for vegetables, and some berry bushes, vines, flowers, and shrubs.[34] The trees and plants produce bountiful harvests that are healthy and delicious. Growing our own food is optimal, because the inherent intelligence in plants will, with time, attune itself to us as their caregivers and benefactors, and the fruits and vegetables they provide will tend to become, as people of earlier times understood, increasingly more tailored specifically for us, and become not just nutritional but also medicinal. The ancient wisdom of conscious gardening has unfortunately been suppressed and mostly lost, but we can experiment and learn about the many benefits of growing our own food as a meditation on lovingkindness and on the interconnectedness of living systems.[35]

We can also support local farmers through farmers' markets and through buying cooperatives, community-supported agriculture (CSAs),[36] and local grocery stores. As we get to know local farmers, we can be increasingly assured of providing high-quality foods for our families. Relying on unprocessed or minimally-processed organic foods, with at least half live and uncooked, our food is vibrantly nutritive and it becomes simple and straightforward to thrive as vegans. Creating meals from a modest variety of whole grains, vegetables, seeds, beans, nuts, fruits, herbs, spices, mushrooms, sprouts, and starches, it is not difficult or complicated to eat a nutritious and delicious diet. In our world today, it is essential to proactively prioritize organically-grown whole plant-sourced foods as the solid foundation for radiant health.

Also, over the past forty years of vegan living, it has become clear that food is not the only factor in determining the quality of our health, and that most of the health problems that vegans have can be traced to non-food causes, or to eating plant-based foods that are highly processed or non-organic. Many processed vegan foods are unhealthy, and while they can sometimes make transitioning from meat, dairy, and eggs more comfortable and familiar, it is best to quickly adopt a diet consisting primarily of whole, organic plant-sourced foods.

On one level, our body is a biochemical system, and foods containing white flour, white sugar, white rice, processed oils, salt, packaged foods, genetically-engineered foods, chemical residues, artificial flavors and preservatives, dough conditioners, and other toxic ingredients and residuals all need to be cleansed from our system, and tend to cause a variety of symptoms. If we stick to organic unprocessed whole foods, our body has less cleansing to do, and these foods, as the research of Dr. T. Colin Campbell has revealed, have a symphonic effect, with the remarkable intelligence and vitality inherent in these foods supporting each other and our living systems and cells as well.[37] Additionally, it seems to be helpful to include plenty of uncooked foods, which are especially rich in fiber and nutrients.

Starch is our good friend and provides us with clean-burning energy, so organic sweet potatoes, potatoes, and squashes, as well as grains, pastas, legumes and some vegetables are valuable sources of the healthy complex carbohydrates we refer to as starches.[38] Non-starchy vegetables, greens, sprouts, fruits, berries, and mushrooms are robust sources of complex carbohydrates and phytonutrients. Naturally-occurring oils and essential fatty acids can be found in all plant-sourced foods, and especially concentrate in nuts, seeds, and legumes. Minimizing the intake of processed oils is very helpful, because these are typically highly refined and can harm the body in its attempt to metabolize them.

It's generally best to eliminate or at least significantly reduce three of the major components of unhealthy and addictive processed foods: salt, oil, and sugar. The so-called SOS-free diet liberates us from these ubiquitous non-foods.[39] Salt tends to dehydrate us, and commercial salt can be filled with toxins and chemicals to improve its pourability. It's best to sparingly ingest only high-quality, minimally processed salt that contains a wide variety of minerals besides sodium.[40] Oils are virtually always highly processed and can be eliminated or replaced with avocadoes, nuts, seeds, or tahini mixed with water, or with vinegar, or fresh lemon or orange juice, for example. We humans are designed for and thrive on large amounts of fiber and with significantly less oils and fats than we find in the Standard American Diet. Finally, refined sugar is now well-recognized to be a harmful and addictive toxin that similarly finds its way into most processed foods. Reducing salt intake also tends to reduce potential cravings for sugar, alcohol, and caffeine and vice-versa.[41]

How We Eat and Prepare Food

Vegan nutrition is actually simple, and we can easily partake of the huge array of plant-sourced foods and thrive, as long as we stay away from processed and non-organic foods. While eating a wide variety of foods is often recommended, people in many cultures have flourished on plant-sourced diets that were quite limited by what crops they were able to grow, because our bodies are adept at recycling nutrients if they are not in abundance in the foods we are eating. There is tremendous intelligence in our body. The main reason hospitals are filled is because we overwhelm our body with toxins, saturated fats, and inflammatory animal proteins, and we disconnect from the other keys to healthy living. The well-known Ayurvedic proverb sums it well: "When diet is wrong, medicine is of no use. When diet is right, medicine is of no need."

According to John McDougall, MD, and many other health researchers, an optimal ratio percentage of carbohydrates, protein, and fats, in terms of caloric intake, is 80-10-10.[42] Research is clear that people in cultures eating high complex-carbohydrate, low-protein diets have the greatest longevity and least amount of chronic disease.[43] Besides what we have briefly covered—eating plenty of starch and complex carbohydrates for our energy requirements, not worrying about protein because virtually all plant foods are sources of adequate protein, and getting our fats primarily from nuts, seeds, olives, avocadoes, and other whole foods—an essential and neglected aspect of eating is our attitude while doing so. In other words, besides being mindful of what we are eating, it is helpful to be mindful of how we are eating, and to take time to chew our food thoroughly, and to eat in an undistracted and relaxed manner.[44] In many traditional cultures, people understand that it is best to cultivate an attitude of appreciation while we are eating, and to keep our thoughts in harmony, and free of the disturbances of the outer world.

The Zen-inspired meals served in Japanese tea ceremonies epitomize this spirit, emphasizing the importance of serenity and beauty, as well as deep appreciation for the tastes, textures, aromas, and flavors of the foods and beverages, and the thoughtfulness of the cook and host. The idea is to look deeply into the foods we are eating, and into where they came from, and how they arrived in our kitchen, and on our plate, and through this practice, to connect more fully with the essence of the foods, and with the farmers and others involved, and with the sun, rain, soil, gardens, orchards, and the natural world, and beyond that, to honor and appreciate the transcendent dimension that is the source of our life and of all life. Eating has been recognized from ancient times as a sacred ritual where what is "not-me" becomes "me," and is thus deserving of our utmost attention, awareness, and respect. With this understanding, we see the sacred nature of food, and the importance of never wasting it.

There is an old Zen story that illustrates this. Once upon a time in ancient China, a young man who yearned for spiritual enlightenment heard of a great Zen master who lived on a far-away mountain. He made the long journey and as he was finally walking up the path to this master's temple, he saw, to his great dismay, a cabbage leaf floating down the stream that ran beside the path. The fact that the monks in the kitchen were so undisciplined and unaware that they allowed a cabbage leaf to float down the stream caused him to seriously doubt the depth of wisdom of the Zen master whom he had journeyed so far to see. As he was about to turn around and leave in deep disappointment, he heard a sound, and looking up, he saw the temple cook running down along the stream to retrieve the wayward cabbage leaf. The sincerity and diligence of the cook assured him that the temple master was great in his wisdom and awareness, after all. As the old saying goes, we can judge a spiritual teacher by the quality of the teacher's students.

Eating together mindfully is cross-culturally understood to be the foundation of maintaining healthy families and relationships. The tendency in modern societies to throw food away, and to eat while watching television, while texting, while driving, while doing a business deal, while arguing, and while upset, are all based on a failure to understand the symphonic nature of food and our bodies. Digesting and assimilating food requires and is affected by a wide variety of hormones and enzymes, and our emotions and state of mind also influence the release of these substances in our body. Eating slowly, cultivating gratitude, and enjoying the food and friendly conversation with others, and the beauty around us, are all important aspects of healthy assimilation and living.

Additionally, our attitude while preparing food is significant. Asian cultures traditionally teach, for example, that besides material sustenance, food is also a vehicle for vital energy, known as *prana* (Sanskrit) or *chi* (Chinese), and that while we are preparing food, we are contributing our unique energy to the food, of which everyone will partake. For this reason, only seasoned monks who were experienced meditators were allowed to prepare food in the Zen monasteries, because it was understood that food prepared in an agitated or distracted state of mind can negatively influence the energy of the food and be disturbing to those eating it. This is another strong reason to avoid foods cooked and prepared in fast-food situations by disgruntled personnel, or in industrial factories by automated machines. As the saying has it, we are what we eat, and ill-tempered, unhealthy, artificial foods tend to create similar people.

Finally, it is also important to be aware of the quality of the pans and other implements we are using when we cook, prepare, and store the food we are eating. As mentioned earlier, while we have found that eating at least fifty or sixty percent of food uncooked is beneficial, we have also come to realize that when we are cooking vegetables, potatoes, rice, pasta, beans, and other foods, most commercial types of cookware leach metallic and chemical toxins into the food. This is of course especially true of pans coated with Teflon and other non-stick films, as well as aluminum pans, which leach harmful chemicals and aluminum. Even Pyrex glass contains toxic metals, as do cast iron, ceramic, and stainless-steel pans. These metallic residues end up in our food as the pans are heated, and water and oil pull them out and into our food.

Fortunately, surgical steel and titanium pans alleviate this problem, and although they are more expensive, they seem much more durable as well; for example, ours are now 25 years old and they still look like new.[45] We have met people whose chronic disease disappeared simply by exchanging their cookware for higher quality, non-toxic pans. Additionally, plastics often contain bisphenols, such as BPA and BPS, which are known endocrine disruptors.[46] Aluminum and other metal cans are coated inside with plastic, and we often buy and store foods in plastic, increasing the load of harmful chemicals we need to cleanse from our bodies. The more we can use glass, organic cloth, bamboo, and other nontoxic materials for storing and preparing our foods, the better.

Besides what we eat, how we eat, and in what we prepare and store it, it's helpful to understand how much to eat. Studies consistently show that over-eating is detrimental to health, and that it's helpful to stop eating before full satiation is reached. This is a fine line, and we have found it takes practice. Ample chewing, about forty or fifty times or so before swallowing, improves digestion and bioavailability of nutrients, and also slows down the eating process somewhat, so that it is easier to stop eating before getting too full. The generally high-fiber content of unprocessed plant-sourced foods makes it easier to avoid over-eating because fiber requires more time to chew, and its bulk causes us to feel satiated and to naturally stop eating. It also passes quickly and easily through our system, cleansing as it goes, so we generally feel lighter after eating than when eating animal-sourced foods that are deficient in fiber and filled with heavy and cumbersome fat and protein.

In sum, eat slowly, and explore the benefits of fasting. Many people and cultures have found that it is helpful to fast. This is a large and important topic, which we discuss briefly here, with further information available in the Resources. There are different types of fasting. A relatively easy and surprisingly effective type of fasting is called intermittent fasting, and it consists of simply extending the length of time when our body is not digesting food. The basic idea behind fasting is that when our body is not engaged in digesting foods, it is then free to engage a completely different modality, which is that of cleansing. In modern life, we tend to eat from morning till night, both meals and snacks, so our body may rarely enter the cleansing mode. With intermittent fasting, we consciously refrain from eating anything after the last meal of the day, and extend that time until we "break our fast" with breakfast. So, for example, it has been our practice for many years to finish the last meal by 6:30 p.m., and then not eat anything at all until our morning green smoothie at 10:30 a.m., which gives our body 16 hours every day with no food coming in. Something like this is of course adjustable and is relatively easy and straightforward, and some extend it. For example, when I was living in the Zen monastery in Korea, we followed the Buddhist practice of not eating after noon, and so there were just two meals, with breakfast at 6:00 a.m., for an intermittent fasting regime of 18 hours.

The other type of fasting, which we can undertake for one, two, or three days, up to perhaps a couple of weeks or longer, gives our body a longer and more sustained opportunity to cleanse, and can be remarkably helpful for healing disease and for weight loss and spiritual renewal. There are three main types of fasts: air fasting, which is consuming no food or liquids, water fasting, which is consuming only water (with perhaps some lemon juice in the water as an aid to cleansing) and juice fasting, consuming water plus juices, usually fresh-squeezed vegetable juices, with some fruit juice, and perhaps some vegetable broth. Madeleine and I have tried all three over the years, and have basically found them all to be beneficial.

Air fasting is obviously the most intense, and is typically an adjunct to concentrated spiritual practice, as on a meditation retreat to focus without any distractions, and 24 to 30 hours is typically the most we would go without drinking or eating. Water fasts can be an excellent addition to a health regime because drinking plenty of water helps to flush toxins, and many people find it helpful to water fast one day per week, or three days per month, or one week every year, and so forth. Madeleine and I both did quite a few three- and seven-day water fasts in the early years when we were starting out on our vegan journeys, and we experienced significant benefits while cleansing the toxins we had accumulated in our first twenty or so years of life, during which we had been less conscious in our living habits. We have also found that water fasting in nature is a particularly effective way to spiritually cleanse and deepen our awareness, and that it is important with water fasting that we rest so that our body can metabolize and eliminate excess fat and toxins. If we engage in aerobic exercise while fasting, we can harm the body because it is then forced to burn lean muscle mass.[47] Juice fasting with fresh vegetable juices is helpful in gently and effectively cleansing, while still having energy to carry on our lives normally. It is advisable to study fasting more thoroughly before embarking on a fast,[48] and for those who prefer, there are some institutes and centers that provide supervised fasting.[49]

The basic ideas underlying healthy nutrition are simple and straightforward: in our world today, with petrochemical cartels churning out massive quantities of toxic chemicals, we are called to respond in a proactive way and do our best to consume only organic (preferably veganic), unprocessed whole plant-sourced foods. It's not much more complicated than that, though it's not necessarily easy, given the resistance to both unprocessed and authentically organic foods in most markets and restaurants. Condiments, sauces, herbs, and spices should also be organic and non-irradiated. That's why, again, it is especially helpful to grow as much food as we can ourselves, and carefully read and understand all labels, and get to know some local farmers, if possible, through regional farmers' markets and co-ops.

It is also good to remember that if we are transitioning to a healthy plant-sourced diet, our body will likely go through a cleanse, because organic fruits and vegetables naturally work to detoxify the body. We may experience cleansing symptoms such as diarrhea, coughing, runny nose, headache, skin rashes, and so forth, which are not "sickness," but are evidence of healthy detoxification, and are vehicles through which the body is removing harmful substances that have been sequestered away in fat cells, possibly for years or even decades. The inherent intelligence of our physiology will take advantage of every opportunity to heal and cleanse, and we can cooperate with it most efficiently when we understand what is happening, and don't repress the cleansing by taking chemical drugs or unhealthy foods that short-circuit the process.

The Big Picture of Nutrition

There is quite a bit more to nutrition than just food; we are also called to look into beverages, for example, as well as personal care products, and other aspects of our way of living. The same principles apply that we have been discussing, which are to question cultural norms and corporate advertising, and keep our minds and bodies as free as possible from harmful pollutants that injure and disempower us physically and mentally. For these reasons, Madeleine and I never drink alcoholic beverages of any kind, and have not done so in the last fifty years. Alcohol is a potent toxin; it literally intoxicates. It destroys liver and brain tissues, is powerfully addictive, causes enormous social, financial, and physical damage, and because it is so widely used and accepted, is considered the most harmful drug in our world today.[50] We also have never consumed any soft drinks, coffee, or black tea in the last fifty years. Sodas are filled with toxic chemicals and refined sugar, and may contain caffeine as well, and are linked to obesity and other chronic conditions. Additionally, the substances in sodas, alcohol, coffee, and black tea tend to acidify the tissues, and caffeine is a stimulant that interferes with the body's natural hormonal intelligence. Why do we need something from outside us to stimulate us? We are also careful about commercial health drinks and bottled water, which may have contaminants, and limit processed fruit juices, which tend, even if organic, to have an unnaturally high sugar content. This is true of dried fruits as well, which are typically overly sweet because they are concentrated.

Fresh-squeezed vegetable juices, and fresh-squeezed fruit juices that are mixed with vegetable juices, can be potently healing, and are central to the success of some of the leading alternative healing centers, such as Hippocrates Wellness Institute in south Florida and the Gerson Institute in Baja, Mexico. For example, at Hippocrates, everyone gets an abundant supply of its signature "green drink," which is a blend of four organic juices: celery, cucumber, sprouted sunflower, and sprouted pea. While visiting and teaching there, we have seen people reverse cancer, heal arthritis, get off their diabetes medications, and lose significant weight, making it clear that the living foods and green juice, combined with movement, education, and positive mental attitude, can have a remarkably salutary effect.

In general, the ideal human beverage is "Adam's Ale," our old friend, water. Water is the essence of biological life, and a major key to radiant health is maintaining our body in a well-hydrated state. Water is also profoundly mysterious, with some researchers discovering that it also has the capacity to hold and transmit information and states of consciousness.[51] Our bodies are three-quarters water, and eating foods that are water-rich, like vegetables, berries, fruits, herbs, and sprouts, makes it easier to stay hydrated, and when these foods are grown and prepared with love and care, the water in the foods may be imparting this consciousness to us when we eat them.

From this metaphysical perspective, we can also better understand the toxic effects of animal-based and factory-produced foods that contain water that has been saturated with terror, trauma, and toxic poisons, and also regimented and industrialized in unnatural ways. How does it affect our cells to be constituted by brutality and mechanization? Our blood vessels, continually carrying nutrients to all 30 trillion cells, and removing toxins and waste products, do so through a water-based delivery system that is about 60,000 miles long, more than twice the circumference of the Earth. Every cell is bathed in a

water-based solution, and researchers now liken the com-
plexity of each individual cell to a large city, so it is easy
to see that the amount of universal intelligence invested
in each one of us is incalculably vast, and it is sobering to
realize that this is also true for every bird, fish, and mam-
mal as well, including the pigs, chickens, cows, and other
animals we routinely exploit and kill for food.

Because water is the universal solvent, virtually all
the toxins spewed by industries, agriculture, and modern
life eventually end up in water, so a filter that removes
chemicals, heavy metals, fluoride, and prescription drug
residues is essential. Distillation is the most thorough,
though it also removes all minerals as well. Reverse osmo-
sis and carbon block filters have the capacity to remove
most pollutants, and there are a number of filters on the
market from which to choose, both for home installation
and travel.[52] Besides filtering water, we feel it's helpful to
structure the water also. Water typically travels long dis-
tances through pipes and tubes before it emerges from
faucets. This unnatural process tends to bind the water
molecules tightly together so that the water is not easily
assimilated by our tissues and by the plants in our gardens. To help remedy this, water structuring devices rep-
licate the natural swirling action found in streams and
rivers. They are available both for travel and for permanent installation in home and garden water systems. We
have found that our fruit trees, berries, herbs, and vegetables need less of this structured water, and we also seem
to drink less to stay hydrated.[53]

We have been discussing nourishment by food and
water, but air is obviously the most essential nutrient,

without which we cannot live for more than a few short minutes. We may eat one or two liters of food daily, and drink three or four liters of water, but every day we breathe about 11,000 liters of air. While toxic pollutants in our food and water are important issues, air pollution has a tremendous potential to contribute to disease as well. Our liver does its best to remove the over 80,000 registered man-made chemicals that can find their way into our bloodstream through food, water, air, skin, and injections, and the more we can consciously minimize our exposure to these chemicals, the better. If we live in an urban area or an area near a road, factory, farm, or other source of air pollution, we should consider using a HEPA filter to remove the PM2.5 particles that are harmful to our health.

Besides these outside sources of air pollution, there is indoor air pollution caused by the outgassing of formaldehyde, flame retardants, and other chemicals from carpets, particle board, cabinets, furniture, bedding, appliances, cleaners, paints, and so forth, and possibly radon gas from under home foundations. Forced-air heating and air conditioning dry out the air, generate harmful positive ions, and are best minimized or avoided. Getting an air quality detector may be helpful, and making it a habit to open the windows several times daily to refresh the air is also helpful. It goes without saying that directly inhaling toxic smoke and gases, as in vaping and smoking tobacco and cannabis,[54] is harmful to lung and circulatory tissues, and as is the case with consuming drugs, a significant burden is placed on our body to cleanse the toxins before they inflict damage.

Sunshine and fresh air are naturally health-promoting, and deep breathing and exercising in areas where we know the air is clean, such as in forests, is a good way to cleanse toxins from our system, expelling them through our breath. Besides taking sun baths, where we soak in the rays of the sun, preferably with little or no clothing on, and allow the healing energy of the sun full access to every part of our skin, we can also take air baths, especially if the sun is too intense. We can be in the shade, preferably in a natural area where the air is clean and there is a breeze. For example, health researchers in Japan have discovered that engaging in "forest therapy"—simply being in a forested area for several hours—significantly improves overall wellness.[55]

Air is filled with energy, and deep conscious breaths that fill our diaphragm are integral not only to inner peace but to vitality and health. Our culture, however, encourages shallow chest breathing, and this has been linked to anxiety and low energy. Learning to breathe properly—mindfully and deeply—contributes significantly to radiant health and mental relaxation. Yawning is also unfortunately suppressed in our society, and yawning, especially full free-spirited yawns coupled with stretching, is important in oxygenating our blood and vitalizing our body and mind.

Another key to radiant health is being aware that our skin is permeable, and avoiding applying anything to it that we wouldn't eat. Just as the food industry employs armies of scientists to concoct processed foods using harmful chemicals, preservatives, and artificial colors and flavors in order to market the most profitable products possible—with explosively appealing tastes and textures intended to generate strong customer appeal bordering on addiction—the personal care and home products industries similarly employ legions of scientists and marketing professionals to maximize appeal, consumption, and profits. There is a vast array of these products today, including toothpastes, skin creams, perfumes, shampoos, lipsticks, nail polishes, sunscreens, body washes, deodorants, make-up, hair-color, facials, laundry detergents, fabric softeners, cleansers, dish soaps, and other personal and home care products. Government agencies like the FDA, having been captured by the industries they are supposed to be regulating, provide virtually no protection for consumers of food products from the toxic preservatives and chemicals that end up in foods. For personal and home care products, there is even less protection. It is basically non-existent, as the documentary *Stink!* demonstrates.[56] For example, when a product lists the word "fragrance" on its list of ingredients, that one word can be a placeholder for any number, even hundreds, of toxic chemicals and carcinogenic substances that the manufacturer is not required to disclose to consumers, under the guise that they are trade secrets.

Fortunately, we can patronize companies making organic vegan and chemical-free shampoos, creams, detergents, and other products if we are willing to research their ingredients. We list some in the Resources section. We can also simply refrain from using some products. For example, we don't have to necessarily buy and use sunscreen, deodorant, skin cream, nail polish, perfume, toothpaste, window cleaner, laundry detergent and cleansers. For laundry detergent, Madeleine and I mainly use soap nuts (that grow on trees in India),[57] we make our own toothpaste, combining baking soda, sea salt, and peppermint oil, we use baking soda and vinegar for general cleaning, a good microfiber cloth and water works wonders on windows, deodorant is typically unnecessary on a clean vegan diet, as is soap, except perhaps after doing greasy mechanical work. Soaps destroy the natural and beneficial oil layers on the skin and scalp. Sunscreens are notoriously toxic, and mostly unnecessary if we eat a healthy diet avoiding trans fats, because the free radicals caused by trans fats in our skin cells make our skin susceptible to skin cancer when exposed to the sun. Instead of lathering on toxic sunscreen to protect ourselves from skin cancer, we can clean up our diet, and as we gradually accustom our skin to the sun, it becomes more resilient and the sun becomes our friend, blessing us not just with healthy vitamin D, but with vitality, energy, and perhaps even with information and insights. What we interpret as light and heat from the sun could also be intelligence and information that is healing and supportive of our entire being.

We are also called to be aware that some of the chemical discharges from industry as well as from geo-engineering weather warfare operations may be damaging and depleting layers in the atmosphere that normally protect us from certain harmful ultra-violet and infrared solar radiation. Profits are not made from healthy people, but from sick ones, so it is essential to be proactive, aware, and self-reliant in order to protect our health from the ongoing deliberate chemical, electromagnetic, and informational toxicity being deployed throughout our society. Health is the foundation of freedom and both are our responsibility to safeguard. If we rely on the medical industry to ensure our health, and government and laws to protect our freedom, we will lose both very quickly.

Because of the continual assault of unnatural toxins, it is important to eat cleansing foods on a daily basis, and to engage the many other avenues we have available to us that facilitate cleansing and vitalization of our mind-body, as we discuss throughout this book. For example, as we abandon the processed comfort foods that tend to be addictive, our taste buds change and become more refined, and these healthy foods eventually become comfort foods because we relish not only their delicious, more natural flavors and textures, but also the thought that we are doing our best to take responsibility for our health and to show kindness to others.

Consuming Media

In addition to the quality of our food, water, air, and everything that comes into contact with our skin, and how these affect our health, we also invariably end up consuming media, which can be similarly informative and empowering, or deceptive and debilitating. Mainstream news and information, as well as most Hollywood films and commercial music and television programming fall decidedly into the latter category. A favorite saying, heard often at The Farm community where I lived briefly back in 1975 and became a vegetarian was, "Guard your gourd;" in other words, protect your mind from harmful influences. The quality of our conversations is also a direct form of consumption, and besides our friends, colleagues, and family members, we now also spend unprecedented amounts of time with online personalities, programming, and information on our mobile devices, computers, and televisions.

The power of community is well understood in spiritual traditions, and the important truth is that we become like the people with whom we spend most of our time and with whom we have significant relationships. When formulating a contemporary articulation of the Fifth Precept, which enjoins Buddhists against consuming and distributing toxic drugs and alcohol, Zen master Thich Nhat Hanh explicitly includes toxic media. He calls this precept "The Fifth Mindfulness Training," and his words illuminate the spirit of the practice of deep veganism and of mindful consumption that we are advocating:

> Aware of the suffering caused by unmindful consumption, I vow to cultivate good health, both physical and mental, for myself, my family, and my society by practicing mindful eating, drinking and consuming. I vow to ingest only items that preserve peace, well-being and joy in my body, in my consciousness, and in the collective body and consciousness of my family and society. I am determined not to use alcohol or any other intoxicant or to ingest foods or other items that contain toxins, such as certain TV programs, magazines, books, films and conversations. I am aware that to damage my body or my consciousness with these poisons is to betray my ancestors, my parents, my society and future generations. I will work to transform violence, fear, anger and confusion in myself and in society by practicing a diet for myself and for society. I understand that a proper

diet is crucial for self-transformation and for the transformation of society.[58]

To sum up this section on healthy nutrition, the first
of the six essential practices: an organic plant-sourced
diet of whole, unprocessed foods maximizes nutrients and
minimizes the poisons that concentrate in animal-sourced,
non-organic, and processed foods. An organic vegan diet
of compassion and respect to animals, ecosystems, wildlife, hungry people, and future generations is a primary
key to realizing optimal health and happiness for ourselves and for the environmental and social systems in
which we are embedded. Additionally, it is important to
drink uncontaminated water, so a filter that will remove
fluoride, chlorine, and the other pollutants typically
found in water today is recommended. Proper breathing
of minimally polluted air is essential, as is mindful use of
personal care and cleaning products.

I have found that spiritual teachers are correct in
recommending the abstention from alcohol and drugs,
including caffeine, nicotine, psychotropic substances, and
the corner drug store offerings of pills, sprays, and so forth,
as much as possible. These generally impede and damage
our natural health, and are unnecessary if we are following the guidelines above. Finally, it is essential to refrain
from toxic inner and outer conversations, and from commercial media because of its misleading consumerist and
divisive orientation that is harmful to our understanding,
as well as to our inner harmony and health. When people
ask how it's been possible for Madeleine and me to avoid
visiting drug stores over the past fifty years, we reply that

it's not difficult to explain: we haven't exposed ourselves to TV or radio programming for the past fifty years.

Instead of consuming the generally harmful and deceptive programming of commercial media, we can practice partaking of constructive and inspiring conversations, books, articles, films, music, and alternative media content. Careful discernment is decidedly necessary during these times of media corruption, calling for both critical thinking as well as intuitive sensitivity to the deeper truths in our world. For this, meditation, our next key to health, may be helpful.

Please see Madeleine's Intuitive Kitchen at the beginning of the Resources section of this book for practical meal preparation ideas and shopping tips.

Chapter Two

THE SECOND KEY: MEDITATION AND SPIRITUAL PRACTICE

"There is no salvation in becoming adapted to a world which is crazy."
—HENRY MILLER

"Meditation is not evasion; it is a serene encounter with reality."
—THICH NHAT HANH

"If you decide to not lose your peace, nobody on this earth can make you unhappy or can take your peace away. You are the cause for your peace, for your joy, and for your unhappiness. So let global peace and happiness begin with you."
—SWAMI SATCHITANANDA

The Open Field of Meditation

The second key to healthy living is the natural human capacity to quiet our minds and enter a state of one-pointed, calm, clear awareness. This is usually referred to as meditation, but prayer, especially contemplative prayer, is similar, and implies a consciousness that is quiet and receptive to grace and to insights that flow from beyond the usual self-oriented realm of mental conditioning. Contemporary research demonstrates that this meditative awareness, practiced properly, brings significant physiological and psychological benefits,[59] and ancient wisdom traditions emphasize that cultivating relaxed and focused equanimity is central to liberation and spiritual realization. Our minds, thoroughly programmed and conditioned by our culture, can benefit substantially from a daily practice, preferably early in the morning and again in the evening. Through this, we consistently and rhythmically create a space where our mind can begin to return home to its original state of harmony and presence. We can then bring this quality of inner peace with us into our day, and into our repose at night.

Regular practice connects us with the transpersonal dimension of our being, and with the truth that we are essentially eternal consciousness—beyond birth and death—whole, complete, and free. Outer freedom is ultimately impossible without inner discipline, and requires our ongoing efforts to liberate ourselves from delusions, distractions, and cravings. Meditative efforts assist us in freeing ourselves from the materialist falsehoods our culture injects into all of us from infancy, and from bondage to pride, greed, jealousy, anger, and the other negative emotions that flow from the customary mental habit of contracted separateness. Through the inner silence of meditation, we can realize the interconnectedness of all manifestations of life, and open more fully to our inner guidance system, which continually reveals to us our ever-evolving purpose and helps us understand and realize our creative potential.

Though there are many forms of meditation and prayer, the most important thing is to find one that resonates, and to practice daily. Our entire life can become an extension of our spiritual practice, and every situation can become an opportunity to deepen our understanding of the fundamental interconnectedness of the myriad expressions of life, and of respect and goodwill for all, and to live this more authentically. This path of freedom brings integrity, space, and abundance to our lives. As we free ourselves, our health increases, and we develop the capacity to help others liberate themselves as well.

Meditation is effective because it is a counterbalance to the distracted mentality that is pervasive in contemporary society: rather than trying to attain something or change ourselves or others, it is practicing the art of receptive awareness and one-pointed inner listening, poised in this present moment, the only moment that actually exists. We practice letting go of habitual clinging to past- and future-oriented thinking. This helps us to legitimately connect with our deeper awareness, beyond cultural conditioning, and beyond the habitual mental stories that feed our illusory sense of essential separateness from others and the world. The actual focus of attention can simply be the breath as it flows in our nose, or in the rising and falling of our diaphragm, or it can be an image, or a short prayer, or a mantra, or a word or feeling, such as love, or devotion, or gratitude, or a sense of awareness of divine presence. It can also be a state of attentive listening and inner inquiry into the source of the self, gently watching and letting go of thoughts as they arise.

With regular and committed practice, the distracted and unruly mental habits will gradually be tamed, and then the mind can be trained to be ever more focused, steadily freeing it from the anxiety and distress that flow from and reinforce our sense of disconnectedness from nature and the source of our life. The body and mind are essentially a unity, and as the mind de-stresses, bodily tension is relaxed, freeing up healing power and vitality. The key point is to set aside time regularly every day and practice without fail, whether there seems to be progress or not. Sometimes progress is invisible, and in our busy world, we may be tempted to use our designated practice time to be more busy or seemingly productive, but in the long run, time invested in cultivating mental stillness and clarity is essential, and well spent. Humor, joy, inner freedom, clarity, understanding, patience, and many other qualities of our true nature begin to naturally blossom when we put first things first, and consistently and conscientiously build a foundation for inner cultivation, and make it the primary priority in our life. There is no greater potential ally than our own mind, and besides the seeds we have sown through our thoughts, words, and deeds, our mind—or aspects of it—is the only thing we bring with us when we leave this world.

With time, glimpses of samadhi—one-pointed mental absorption—will occasionally be experienced. When samadhi deepens into a sense of abiding in our true home of relaxed and open awareness, we find fears, worries, regrets, and even physical symptoms effortlessly dissolving in the radiance of the joyful freedom that is ever present as the core of our being. Our body is, in many ways, a manifestation of our consciousness, and purifying our consciousness through meditative practice supports the health of mind and body.

According to ancient wisdom traditions, the experience of samadhi while seated in meditation awakens our awareness, so that when we then go through the activities of daily life, we can extend this and maintain a similar sense of harmonious one-pointed awareness. This then further supports our sitting practice, and the qualitative distinction between the time when we are sitting in meditation or prayer and when we are active begins to dissolve. With practice, we are living ever more continually with an awareness that is flavored by, and colored by, the abiding joy and peace of our true nature. This harmony is actually ever present, helping us to fulfill the Biblical teaching that we "pray without ceasing." Due to our cultural conditioning, we have learned well how to continually block this essential harmony with our ongoing mental commentary of worries, plans, regrets, frustrations, judgments, ambitions, and dramas. It emerges from hiding as we untie and release the mental and emotional knots and blockages that spring from the delusion of identifying with our physical body and memories, and learn to pause the unceasing internal dialogue.

The Zen teaching of the three *nens* or three "thoughts" may shed some light on this. The first nen is the pure awareness of seeing, hearing, smelling, or feeling, and so forth. The second nen is immediately attached to it, and is the sense of "me," that I am seeing, I am hearing, I am feeling. The third nen is the entire complex web of thoughts, feelings, comparisons, memories, and judgments arising from our outer and inner perceptions that creates the ongoing matrix-story of our life and fits everything into our internal paradigms, creating our continuous interpretation of the reality around us. We typically live our entire lives after childhood exclusively in the third nen, not experiencing life directly, but experiencing our continually interpreted and somewhat disconnected mental version of it. Through meditation we can gradually develop the capacity to free our mind from its obsession of judging, naming, self-identifying, and categorizing, and begin to live more in the second nen. This opens the capacity to see and experience more directly and clearly, and with further practice, we may be able to return to the first nen of pure awareness, though this requires disciplined cultivation of ethical purity as well as significant liberation of the mind from cultural indoctrination.

Because the mind and the body are fundamentally not-two, the more our mind is liberated and becomes a clear conduit for unfiltered awareness, the more our body is naturally harmonized and freed from dis-eases and disharmonies. This opens the door to experience the deeper truth that we are essentially spiritual, not material, and the healing effect this has on the body. Mary Baker Eddy, the discoverer and founder of Christian Science, puts it this way, "Become conscious for a single moment that Life and intelligence are purely spiritual—neither in nor of matter—and the body will then utter no complaints. If suffering from a belief in sickness, you will find yourself suddenly well."[60]

The Four Viharas Meditation

There is an enormous variety of specific meditations from the world's wisdom traditions with which we can work to bring healing to our consciousness and to our world. One ancient practice is the Four Viharas, also known as the Four Brahmaviharas or the Four Immeasurables. Originating in ancient India, *vihara* means abode in Sanskrit and this practice focuses on the four aspects of our true home, which are *maitri,* lovingkindness; *karuna,* compassion; *mudita,* unselfish joy; and *upekha,* equanimity. The practice entails consciously engendering each vihara in our mind and heart as we inhale, and radiating it outward into the world to bless others as we exhale, in succession, as love, compassion, joy, and peace. The beauty of this practice is that it can be done for any length of time and virtually anywhere, for example, while driving or standing in line at the post office, or sitting in silent meditation. It not only helps to focus the mind, but also at the same time helps to heal and resolve conflicted emotional states that are often deeply rooted in our past. Breathing and radiating love, compassion, joy, and peace is a practice that is excellent for both beginners as well as seasoned practitioners, and it has a long and rich history of being engaged in by countless people for thousands of years.[61]

In this practice, maitri is a mentality of benevolence and kindness toward all living beings, wishing them happiness and all the causes of happiness. Karuna, compassion, is not only empathy for the suffering of others, but is also the yearning to act to help relieve the suffering of others. Mudita has no equivalent word in English, and refers to a joy that needs no reason in the outer world, and is also specifically the joy that we feel in the joy of others and in the celebration of life around us. Upekha is the profound and immeasurable equanimity of detachment. It is the inner peace that arises from regarding all beings equally, with a sense of good will, and of abandoning preferences and favorites, abiding in the harmonious awareness that is free from grasping and rejecting. By cultivating an awareness of these four aspects of our original nature and radiating them into our body and world, we create a foundation for wisdom, and for further progress in meditative concentration and one-pointedness of mind.

In meditative traditions, samadhi (the focused clarity and relaxed inner peace of one-pointed awareness) and sila (the ethical purity that naturally refrains from any thought, word, or action that is harmful to others) reinforce each other. Ethical behavior is a prerequisite for deep inner contemplation. Harmful and deceptive actions disturb the mind and keep it shallow, busy, and disconnected from its deeper wisdom, and this sets up a vicious cycle leading to further hurtful action and further inner disturbance. This is why ahimsa—nonviolence and lovingkindness—and deep vegan living[62] are essential to spiritual maturity. When we act, speak, or think in ways that reduce others to instruments to be used, we harm others for our benefit, violating our true nature. This estranges us from our inner wisdom, creating mental and emotional turmoil that hinder our ability to abide in inner peace, and it interferes with our efforts to deepen our meditation practice and to mature spiritually.

Practicing the Four Viharas and other meditative and spiritual practices regularly can refine and purify our emotional field, thereby bringing healing to our body and mind, making our lives happier and more harmonious, and bringing more peace into the world. For example, I remember one afternoon when I was a Zen monk in Korea, practicing the Four Viharas along with the Zen practice of inner listening and working on the meditative question, "What is this?" ("What is the source of this I?"). On rare occasions, temple supporters would bring a special gift to the Western monks. Each one of us would get a small cake that we could eat at our leisure. On this particular day, most of the monks ate theirs right away, following lunch, but I decided to put mine into the small wooden locker I had for storing my personal effects. When I came back later with the thought of eating it, and opened my locker, to my great surprise, it was gone. One of my brother monks—I had no idea who—had obviously taken it. The interesting thing was that in that moment, because of my ongoing practice of the Four Viharas, the only action my mind could take was to leap to the third vihara, mudita, which is sympathetic joy. I was suddenly filled with a sense of savoring how enjoyable it must have been for the unknown monk to have had his piece of delicious cake, and then, on top of it, to enjoy another piece as well. I so relished this feeling that there was no inkling of feeling wronged, and never any necessity to work through any feelings of loss, anger, or disappointment. Our mind creates our interpretation of reality, moment after moment.

Neurobiologist Donald Hebbe is known for his discovery that "neurons that fire together, wire together."[63] Thus, the more we cultivate and engage in certain thoughts and feelings, the more the neurons in our brain and nervous system connect and support each other in this behavior. This is one reason why it is important to avoid indulging thoughts and feelings of anger, fear, jealousy, regret, and so forth, and instead make an effort to cultivate gratitude, joy, lovingkindness, and contentment, as well as remorse if we have inappropriately harmed others, and most importantly of all, an attitude of questioning and continually inquiring as deeply as we can into the nature of mind and its perceptions and actions. Mental pathways that build up in consciousness are also reflected in our neurology, and as we all know, affect our health as well. The adage by Steven Covey sums it well: "Sow a thought, reap an action; sow an action, reap a habit; sow a habit, reap a character; sow a character, reap a destiny."[64]

With inner work, we can discover new avenues of awareness, and free ourselves and everyone around us from the burden of being offended, of trying to blame others or to justify our actions, and of having to work to forgive others or ourselves. While we can work hard to get out of the boxes that confine and wound us, we can also realize directly that our true nature can never be in any box, or be confined or harmed in any way. Of course, circumstances arise when the seeming harm is much more serious than a piece of cake, but the underlying principle still applies. With practice and effort, we can broaden and illumine our awareness enough that we can experience, and abide in, states of consciousness that naturally bring humor, freedom, joy, forgiveness, and clarity where normally we would be reacting with fear, anger, sadness, impatience, or retaliatory self-righteousness. Our mind is always creating the context that interprets all experience. As we strive to elevate our mental awareness and to extinguish our identification with the conditioned awareness that revolves perpetually around the false sense of being an isolated self, the whole world changes. The old saying sums it well: "We see things not as they, are but as we are."

Our Heritage of Spiritual Practices

There are literally countless unique prayer and meditation practices that we can explore as part of our human heritage, because all religious traditions and spiritual paths have developed extensive repertoires of practical techniques designed to help us transcend our normal afflicted and limited consciousness. Besides all these spiritual practices from the world's religions, non-religious techniques have been developed by psychologists and by consciousness explorers from many times and places. In addition, we can explore the natural meditative states that occur when we are engaging in things that we love, or that bring us into total involvement, such as certain sports, athletics, dance, yoga, movement, and other physical experiences such as sharing intimacy, engaging in musical and artistic creative expression, and immersing ourselves in nature.

A myriad of prayers, mantras, chants, visualizations, images, contemplations, reflections, disciplines, movements, postures, and breathing practices have been discovered and created to help unify the mind and dissolve our illusions. They all call us, and assist us, to free the mind from the ongoing conditioned internal dialogue that dominates our waking consciousness. Decidedly, meditation is not what we think. It arises as we learn to observe thoughts and feelings, freeing us from the tyranny of conditioned reactivity.

The underlying idea is that when the mind is quiet and clear, like water that has settled and is no longer stirred up and muddy, the self-existent indwelling light naturally begins to penetrate and illumine awareness. From this more relaxed clarity, meditation practices can help us cultivate particular qualities. For example, there is the practice of Taking and Sending, which is done, like many practices, in conjunction with the breathing. As we inhale, we imagine breathing into our heart the suffering and ignorance of others and the world, and then we pause for a moment, and allow our heart to transform this darkness and delusion into the clear white light of joy, freedom, and wisdom. Exhaling, we radiate this light in ever-expanding spheres, sending harmony and healing to every being in the infinite web of relations. This is not considered a beginning practice because we must be confident in our ability to transform the negativity we are inhaling; otherwise, we may begin to take some of it on, which is counterproductive.

The most basic meditation, at the core of all practices, is inner listening, opening to the great inquiry into the source of what we are. This is a direct path, the way of self-inquiry, which calls us to continually deepen our meditative quest to look ever further into whence arises our sense of self, and the awareness that we are experiencing. Just as we have our unique strengths and tendencies, each of us will find the particular practices that resonate with us. Some will be perhaps more devotional, some more investigative, some more service-oriented, and some more inspired by creative impulses. The important factor is perseverance and regularity, as in any endeavor. Committed practice is what brings success. Whatever we practice, we will develop proficiency, whether for good or ill. Though we have unfortunately been compelled to practice emotional and cognitive numbing through being conditioned by, and living in, a society organized around animal agriculture, we can consciously devote ourselves to practicing kindness, sensitivity, and awareness not just in our food and lifestyle choices, but also to go beyond this and undertake the work of inner transformation through spiritual practice.

The research that has been done on meditation over the decades demonstrates that meditation practice can be helpful with physical issues such as blood pressure and other stress-related conditions,[65] as well as with sleep, attention-span, memory, depression, and other mental issues.[66] Of course, there are many other benefits beyond these physical and mental ones, but the main thing to remember is that, like everything else, we get out of anything what we put into it. Essentially, meditation is mindfulness. Mindfulness is the practice of being as conscious as possible at every moment, and as discussed earlier, this ties in well with both spirituality—transcending the delusion of materialism—and deep veganism—looking into our food system and beyond, and honoring the integrity and sovereignty of ourselves and of all living beings. The idea is to practice quieting the mental noise, which is the result of being bombarded from infancy with toxic food, media, drugs, and narratives promoting competition, separateness, and busyness. As we do this, we increasingly reclaim our awake, creative and caring heart-mind in order to unfold our unique gifts, and our mission for contributing to the well-being of others.

Breath Meditation and Sleep Meditation

Our breath is an important ally in this quest because it is the primary ongoing activity that is both conscious and unconscious. By becoming aware of our breathing throughout the waking hours, we begin to elevate and refine our consciousness, and we can also learn to deepen our breathing, and slow it down, which naturally reduces our tendency to reactivity, irritation, and distractedness, and reconnects us with the eternal being that we are, the one for whom our body is breathing, digesting, and in countless ways providing a reliable and valuable vehicle.

There are two basic types of meditation. One is focused-attention practice, in which we develop the mental capacity to maintain one-pointed attention, and the other is open-monitoring practice, in which we engage this undistracted attention to be fully aware of what is arising around us and within us, moment by moment. Both are based on the same principle of cultivating an undistracted clarity of mind, and our breath is central to both. For example, one ancient meditation especially helpful for beginning practitioners is to simply count the inhalations from one to ten, without engaging in discursive thinking, and if we lose track of the count, to just start over, without inner commentary. A variation on this is to count to a hundred and then back to one again, focusing only on the counting. Eventually we can let go of counting and continue to be aware of the breath moving in and out through our nostrils, or in the rise and fall of our diaphragm.

These focused-attention practices develop our familiarity with our mind and the way our focus of attention operates and shifts. They cultivate our ability to be more attentive, conscious, and present. We can also use our breath awareness to practice open-monitoring meditation, as we maintain awareness of the flow of our breath as well as of thoughts and feelings. All of these practices can be done while we are sitting quietly in a meditation session, and also when we are out and about, living our lives. In addition, many specific types of breath practice have been developed over the millennia for specific uses, such as vitalizing the body, calming the mind, synchronizing the brain hemispheres, and so forth.[67]

While breath awareness is an immense and fascinating subject far beyond the scope of this book, it's helpful to be aware of some of the basic techniques, such as square breathing and rebirthing breathing. Square breathing is simply counting the durations of our four breath stages, and having an equal count for each one. For example, we could adopt a count of six for the inhale, the hold, the exhale, and the rest before inhaling again. There are many variations, such as doubling the counts for the second and third stages, the hold and the exhale, or increasing the counts gradually over time. Many people find square breathing and its variations to be helpful in relaxing and focusing. Rebirthing breathing is two-stage, or connected breathing, which is breathing with no delay between inhales and exhales, and it is done with intensity, so that it's helpful to have a partner to monitor our breathing and keep the intensity strong. This practice can be useful in invoking altered states of consciousness and, as the name implies, uncovering deeply buried memories, all the way back to the memory of our birth into this world as a neonate.[68]

Deep, restful sleep can also be seen as a part of our daily prayer and meditation practice, and there are possibilities to use our dream time in ways that bring insight and healing awareness into our lives. This is a vast topic, but in brief, the main keys seem to be to create a healthy sleeping environment, and prepare properly for sleep. We have found that a two- or three-inch thick natural latex rubber mattress is durable and comfortable, with a small organic buckwheat-hull pillow, freeing us from outgassing chemicals, flame retardants, foam, and other toxins. Organic linen or cotton sheets, blankets, and sleepwear, and a bedroom that is completely dark and free of disturbing noise and odors is helpful. Fresh air is also important, so having an open window may be helpful. Some people find that situating the bed so that the head is not to the north is helpful, as well as checking for the presence of ley lines, which are natural earth energy meridians that might be mentally or energetically disruptive.

Additionally, it's advantageous to minimize electromagnetic radiation during our sleep time, and turning off Wi-Fi routers and perhaps looking into ways to shield the bedroom, or getting EMF protecting blankets or devices that can help to reduce the harmful effects of now virtually ubiquitous EMF fields.[69] Some people find earthing sheets that can be energetically grounded are helpful. Using blue-light-blocking glasses in the evening for computer work is advantageous for restful sleep, as is refraining from computer and phone use for an hour or more before going to bed. We typically spend the hour prior to retiring for the night, for example, meditating together, and then I play the piano while Madeleine does gentle ball-dancing exercise[70] and stretching, followed by meditative listening to the music. We sometimes share spiritually inspirational reading together, and then enter the sleep state as consciously as possible. This can include reviewing the day, and giving thanks for the many opportunities and learning experiences we've had. In the morning, after meditation, we share our dreams and work with them individually if we feel so called. Dreams have been a source of insight, inspiration, and learning for countless people for thousands of years, and we can learn to work with dreams, and to get guidance from them, as well as to develop the ability to wake up in our dreams, which is known as lucid dreaming.[71] With practice, we learn more deeply how our waking reality, like the reality we perceive in our dreams, is an arising in our consciousness. We project, as well as witness, both the dreams at night and the waking life that we experience.

It's helpful, during the night, if we awaken and like to return to sleep, to practice the two-step meditative technique of first, consciously relaxing the whole body, and second, letting go of any thoughts so the mind is silent. I've found sleep is virtually certain to come quickly when doing this. We find that six and a half to seven hours is plenty of time to be in bed at night, and rising early before dawn is delightful. Madeleine is especially enthusiastic about the benefits of a mid-day power rest, which is different from a nap in that it is brief, only ten to twenty minutes, and done on one's back. She has found that these power rests are remarkably refreshing, and she combines it with listening to recorded spiritual teachings as she enters the rest.[72]

Though we have only scratched the surface of this vast subject of meditation and prayer, we can see that cultivating a quiet and receptive inner environment is a particularly essential key to physical, psychological, and spiritual health. It is a practice of returning home to our true nature as clear, awake, and conscious beings, and provides the foundation for facilitating the crucial process of freeing ourselves from cultural indoctrination. This does not mean it is a cure-all. It is possible to meditate regularly and fail to seemingly get the desired results due to a variety of factors, usually having to do with a lack of earnestness, or reluctance in following through, and failing to make a sufficient effort to bring meditative awareness and ethical living into the various aspects of our lives. Receiving proper guidance, and understanding the wisdom teachings accurately, are also important.

Ultimately, every honest effort that we make in the direction of compassion, healing, and spiritual liberation is a step toward increasing inner wisdom, the most valuable and positively transformational quality to which we can aspire. Effort and discipline are essential, and grow naturally as we realize the joy and freedom they confer. Discipline should perhaps therefore be spelled "blisscipline." Inner and outer harmony depend on what we are actually practicing throughout our day.

Meditation is extraordinarily simple and straightforward, and because of this we find it profoundly difficult. As a result of our cultural conditioning, we have become complicated and distracted. Meditation aims to cultivate pure awareness, free from any interference by the illusory thief of egocentricity that steals the present moment, and with this theft, diminishes our life, our freedom, our health and happiness, and everything else. As mindfulness, it goes hand-in-hand with spirituality and with deep vegan living, beckoning us toward a positive future that is an ever-present possibility. Doing our best to purify our mind and actions for the benefit of others brings peace and happiness to our heart. Through this cultivation of mindfulness, we naturally activate intuitive insights, and our lives increasingly contribute not only to rescuing animals, nature, and humanity from the harm inflicted by self-oriented misunderstanding, but also to reclaiming harmony for all of us.

The Shining Mind and the Wandering Mind

This mind of infinite brightness,
Clear, free, and unimpeded,
This shining mind sets all the world ablaze.
Joy-filled and quiet,
It spreads from shore to shore,
And covers the lowest valleys and highest mountains.

The old wandering mind
Runs to and fro,
Pacing restlessly back and forth in its cage,
Always searching, thinking, questing,
Always proving, circling, approving and disapproving.
Faster and faster it churns,
Whirling in its endless searching.
How does its head fly off?
How does it burst like a bubble, this wandering mind?

The shining mind is ever at peace,
Serene, calm, and bright,
It sees the world with clear compassion.
Eyes relaxed and twinkling,
Eternally laughing,
This shining mind covers the whole world!

There is nothing to accomplish,
Nothing to prove, and no one to convince of anything.
The shining mind is ever rejoicing, and thus
The wandering mind is settled, at home, and stirs no
more.

This is the way which is not a way.
The shining mind shines and IS—
Vast love fills the universe.

Chapter Three

THE THIRD KEY: HEALTHY RELATIONSHIPS AND COMMUNICATION

"Whatever joy there is in this world, all comes from desiring others to be happy,
And whatever suffering there is in this world, all comes from desiring myself to be happy."
—SHANTIDEVA

"Only when we have become nonviolent toward all life will we have learned to live well ourselves."
—CESAR CHAVEZ

"Freedom and love go together. To love is to not ask anything in return, not even to feel that you are giving something. And it is only such love that can know freedom."
—J. KRISHNAMURTI

The Benefits of Healthy Relationships

The third key to healthy living is taking responsibility for the quality of our relationships and communication. Studies support the truth that we know in our bones: our emotions have an enormous impact on our health. Our relationships and our emotions are deeply connected, and unresolved anger, jealously and other conflicted mind-body states arising out of our relationships call out for healing, and can help us discover pathways to a positive transformation in how we view and relate with others.

For the most part, it seems that we are taught the opposite of authentic and healthy relationships and communication in our society, so quite a bit of both learning and unlearning is essential. Honest, responsible, and loving communication is the foundation of harmonious and enriching relationships with others, and it finds a solid foundation in the first two keys, nutrition and meditation. These can help us to establish our body and mind in a more healthy and harmonious state, which naturally enables us to become more sensitive and respectful in our communication with others. Healthy communication is based on our ability to listen openly and deeply. This often means learning to listen and hear beyond the outer words to the deeper meaning a person is trying to convey. This kind of listening builds trust and respect, and we humans are deeply wired to return to others what we receive. If we want people to listen deeply to us, and to be honest with us, the best way to receive this is to offer it to them. Honesty with others is an outcome of living authentically, and it is an expression of love that brings freedom and clarity.

It is helpful to understand that we have all been born into a culture that tends to indoctrinate us into habitual styles of communication that are often manipulative and aggressive in a variety of ways. Subtle competitive pressures can build up when we are vying with each other to be the center of attention, each of us doing what we can to manipulate the conversation back to us. As a culture, we are so hungry for others who will listen attentively to us that we have created high-priced professionals to fulfill that need. Through deep veganism and meditation, we can begin to recognize and let go of these unhealthy and self-centered habits based on insecurity, and create new ways of relating based on inclusivity, respect, and open-hearted listening. It is through deep listening that we hear the cries of anguish in cheeseburgers and fish sticks, and we can similarly hear the pleas for understanding and recognition hidden within the human communications we are receiving. As we bring our lives into alignment with our values, we learn to refrain from anger, judgment and deceptiveness the same way we refrain from buying and eating meat and dairy products. All are cut from the same cloth: the mentality of exclusion.

The path to happiness is the path of inclusion. Sending cards of gratitude and emails of support, speaking words of encouragement, honestly and lovingly sharing our truth, and keeping our word: these demonstrate our commitment and our respect, and help to bring happiness to others. Ultimately, the most precious "possession" any of us has is the quality of our relationships. These bring us, as we know in our bones, our most valued joys and most searing pains. Building the tower of our relationships with bricks of loving and forthright communication is sure to bless us and everyone many times over. Words are potent, and actions usually even more so. Every day we plant seeds for future experiences not just for ourselves, but for others as well, and these seeds may grow and spread far more than we realize.

For example, back around 1993 when Madeleine and I first married and were living together in a little house two miles out on a dirt road in the hills of northern California, we would occasionally get into misunderstandings that would make it hard to communicate because of our hurt feelings. One evening when this happened, I really wanted to reach out to Madeleine with a few loving words, so I wrote her a note but, because I couldn't bring myself to hand it to her, I spontaneously fashioned it into a paper airplane and sailed it over to her where she was sitting at her desk. Fortunately, she was touched and amused by the flying love note, and so from time to time in those first years we would send each other paper airplane notes as the need arose.

Fast forward 24 years to November of 2017, when Madeleine and I were in Guangzhou, China, where I was lecturing on the main ideas in *The World Peace Diet*, and giving piano concerts, accompanied by slides of Madeleine's paintings and sometimes by her accompaniment on the silver flute as well. The roughly 500 people in the audience became intrigued by what seemed to them to be our remarkably happy and loving relationship, and so we were asked at one point to speak for twenty minutes or so on the stage about what we had discovered to be the secrets to harmonious relationships. We shared our insights and experiences, including the benefits of daily meditation and spiritual practice, healthy plant-sourced meals lovingly prepared and eaten together, and sharing a common mission in our life together. At one point, Madeleine also mentioned briefly in passing how, in the beginning of our relationship when things got a bit difficult, I had sent a paper airplane love note to her. We ended the evening playing some music together, and the next morning took the train to the city of Nanchang for the following day's lecture event on our tour.

When we arrived at the venue that evening, there were again about 500 seats in the theater, and we noticed that every seat had a little table next to it, and every table had a small cup for tea that would be served during the event, and also a paper airplane! Volunteers had apparently heard of our airplane story from the people in Guangzhou, and had made hundreds of paper airplanes so everyone had one, but no one said a word to us about them. During the evening program, we spontaneously decided that it would be lively if everyone took their airplane and wrote a "love note" of appreciation or encouragement and sailed their plane to another member of the audience. Since paper airplanes are inherently wild and erratic in their flights, the recipient would be unpredictable.

How the attendees delighted in doing this! And re-doing it. We enjoyed participating as well and savoring the joy of spontaneous, loving actions. For the rest of the evening, during the lecture and songs, paper airplanes with loving words were sailing silently back and forth throughout the hall. During the grand finale, which was a traditional Chinese large group song, suddenly a few hundred more paper airplanes appeared, and were sent sailing to and fro among the laughing, singing, and dancing crowd.

It brought tears to my eyes, as I reflected on my memory of that night two dozen years ago, when my heart ached, and I felt rejected, alone, and hurt, and somehow found it within myself to send a little paper airplane note to my likewise hurting partner, and how that tiny seed, after 24 years of quietly incubating, suddenly erupted on the other side of the world in a massive action of 500 people joyfully celebrating the power we all have to reach out with love, creativity, and forgiveness, and send each other flying love notes. It is essential that we learn to respect the power of our intentions and actions, even apparently small ones, because they can be amplified and spread far more than we realize throughout the infinite web of relations, returning to us and touching countless beings in ways impossible to foretell.

Disease as Conflict Residue

It is well understood that relationship conflicts, resentments, frustration, and stress often turn inward and harm our physical bodies, sometimes quickly, and sometimes gradually over many years. We are always planting seeds in the universal field of thoughts, words, and deeds, and like mighty trees that grow from small seeds, these also grow over time, and we reap the consequences. Spirituality and deep vegan living are manifestations of planting seeds of love and caring, and when we plant the seeds with our whole heart, and for the best for everyone, they will burst forth in glorious and unexpected ways, bringing healing and happiness in ways we might seldom imagine. Ancient wisdom traditions and contemporary research agree that our health and happiness arise from continually tossing the little paper airplanes of our caring and kindness into the world. The universe notices and remembers everything, and our seeds eventually sprout, perhaps in guises and dimensions of which we are unaware. Every moment is an opportunity, and even when alone, we can deepen our relationships with others and with ourselves, and bring healing into our lives.

As another example, I remember when I was about 25 years old and living in a Tibetan Buddhist meditation center in San Francisco, and decided to undertake a four-month meditation retreat in a tiny meditation cabin deep in an Oregon forest that was built for that purpose by students at the center. Alone there during the rainy winter, it was a time of complete isolation, with absolutely no human contact, during which I engaged in a strict schedule of meditation and traditional prostration practice, staying always within the seven-foot by eleven-foot cabin and its little porch and outside toilet. About two months or so into the retreat, as I was doing hundreds of prostrations daily, I suddenly got an acute pain in my lower back. I could barely move or bend forward without sharp pain. When it became time to sleep for the night, I prayed that in the morning, the pain would be gone. Upon arising, immediately there was again the shooting pain, and I sat down on my meditation cushion for the morning meditation while it was still dark. During the meditation,

I heard a voice speak clearly into my mind these words: "A pain in the body is a pain in the mind," engraving them indelibly into my consciousness.

Contemplating these words, I eventually arose and sat on the bed and began writing in my journal in order to understand what the words signified in this case. I was aware that whenever I bent forward, in order to reach out to get something or do something, the pain flared up. As I wrote about this, engaging in the practice of automatic writing, just allowing words to flow without editing them, it all started to become crystal clear. I could see myself as a little boy, exuberant and filled with energy and curiosity, unabashedly reaching out and exploring the world around me. And then I saw the little boy later, in youth, becoming unsure and reserved, and hesitant to reach out to life for fear of being wounded or criticized. Because I had spent the past two months in intensive meditation and was in an unusually expanded state of consciousness, it was easy to not only understand the youth's pain and reluctance, and have compassion for him, but also to realize the illusory nature of these old wounds. Opening to a rising awareness, I was filled with the understanding that these past wounds and delusions that confined the youth of my past needed no longer to negatively influence the being now writing in the journal.

As I continued with the writing, this expansive feeling and awareness kept growing until it felt all-pervasive and I knew in my bones that though I loved the child and the youth of my past, I was no longer bound by their limitations. I still clearly remember the certainty I felt as I put the journal aside, stood up, and reached out and picked up the water jug on the floor. There was absolutely no pain. It was healed, and there was no surprise about it. In fact, it seemed like no big deal. A pain in the body is a pain in the mind. When we resolve our inner mental and emotional pains, our body will tend to return to harmony and refrain from complaining.

Of course, if instead of introspecting my back pain, I had gone to a doctor and gotten a medication for pain, or had gone in for surgery, the underlying causal condition would continue to be unaddressed, and quite likely none of the medical interventions would have resolved the problem, or if they succeeded in masking the symptoms, they would have merely driven the unfaced pain deeper, and it would perhaps have then manifested as something else, such as cancer, heart disease, or a so-called accident.

By making the inner efforts, and looking beyond the outer material façade of life—into the living truth of our reality as expressions of awareness manifesting temporarily through an apparent form—we can turn the seemingly negative experiences in our life into valuable opportunities for reclaiming a more conscious and love-filled life. At the end of the four months, as I left the little cabin and walked back down the trail in the drizzly forest, the sound of a dog barking suddenly catapulted me up and out of the body in a momentary and timeless experience of floating amid the trees and watching the body walking down the path in the woods. The most essential key to radiant health and happiness is deepening our understanding that we are not merely this body, nor this collection of thoughts, feelings, beliefs, memories, and experiences.

The materialist narrative at the core of our culture, thriving on animal agriculture, reduces us all to material objects, and this delusion is the root of our pervasive confusion, and of the disharmonies in our relationships, bodies, and psyches. We have all been wounded, starting with our birth, and perhaps in the womb as well, by the variety of harsh and toxic attitudes, foods, narratives, chemicals, and customs that are practiced in our culture. There is structural violence in the way mothers and babies are treated in the birthing process itself, and in the early months and years of life following. In many ways, it is modeled on a dairy operation, where technology and ownership priorities take precedence over bonding and nurturing. A glimpse of this appeared in a video during the Covid era when a pregnant woman in a hospital was debating a hospital administrator about having her newborn vaccinated, and the administrator said, "As long as the baby is inside you, it's your baby, but when it comes out, it's not yours anymore."

On a dairy, as in all herding operations, both mothers and their offspring are routinely reduced to commodity objects. Virtually all of us are participating in this by consuming foods and other products that harm and exploit animals, and we inevitably reap what we sow. Healthy, liberating, and empowering human relationships ultimately require that we transform our food and consumption patterns, and stop exploiting animals. This helps us to heal our culturally-ingrained disconnectedness, and by embracing a practice of treating all apparent others, both animal and human, with respect and kindness, we can increasingly savor the harmony, fulfillment, and mind-body vibrancy that this brings into our lives and all our relationships.

Understanding that we have all been wounded from infancy can help us have compassion and understanding for others in our relationships with them, rather than judgment and hostility. Wounded people tend to wound other people, and understanding this can help us to refrain from taking things personally. In many ways, we have all been culturally conditioned from our earliest moments. Our actions, reactions, and habits, if we are not connected with our intuition and deeper awareness, are to a large degree a direct result of this conditioning.

There is an illustrative metaphor from the Taoist tradition. A man is on a lake, lying on his back on the floor of a little boat, dreamily enjoying the beautiful sky and clouds. Suddenly he is jolted hard as another boat rams into his! Immediately, he's furious. Who could be so stupid or malicious to aggressively slam into his boat like that? Jumping up, he is ready to righteously express his anger, but instead he starts laughing merrily: the boat is empty. It was just drifting, propelled by winds and currents. This teaching has been an enormous help over the years. In many ways, when it comes to relationships in our human world, there are a lot of empty boats, propelled by unseen winds and currents. We are all wounded from infancy, both individually and collectively, due simply to being born into, and required to embrace and participate in, a culture organized around oppressing animals and the sacred feminine. As infants and children, we are defenseless to the harmful impacts and abuses embedded in our culture's food rituals, medical system, educational system, media, and other institutions. More than we typically realize, we are propelled by cultural conditioning that is deeply embedded and largely unconscious. This awareness can help us have understanding for one another. Those of us who are moved to harm ourselves and others are often driven by forces we don't understand, and of which we are not aware.

With this understanding, we can also make a more conscious effort to take responsibility for our relationships and counteract and heal our culture's woundedness by proactively conveying love and appreciation to others. Smiling—and expressing kindness, friendliness, cheerfulness, and gratitude—creates a foundation for healthy family and community life. For example, research validates what we already know intuitively, that the quality of our communication directly affects the health of our relationships. According to studies, when the ratio of positive (expressing appreciation and support) to negative (criticism and judgment) communications is fifty-fifty, marriages end in divorce virtually 100 percent of the time. A ratio of 70/30 gives better results, but stable and satisfying marriages typically have a ratio of about 80/20 or 90/10.[73] We can each be proactive and make an effort to provide at least ten compliments for every critique, and bring more lovingkindness into our world. Everyone we meet is working with difficult issues of which we know little, perhaps struggling and feeling alone, and when we reach out with caring words and gestures, we sow seeds of both inner harmony and world peace.

Reciprocity is a fundamental underlying principle in human consciousness and relationships, and this is visible in mammalian species in general. Our relationships are propelled by our responses to the words and actions of others, and there are potent drives in us to reciprocate a favor with a favor, a gift with a compliment, an insult with an act of revenge, and so forth. We can practice being proactive rather than merely reactive, and as Jesus wisely counseled, return anger and hatred with forgiveness and lovingkindness. Our relationships may seem to be with other people, but it may be more correct to view our relationships as being more accurately with ourselves, and also with the one life that lives through all of us. Whatever seeds we sow, the universe will reciprocate. It may or may not be through the particular individuals we believe are involved because the movie of our life and being is much larger, and nothing is hidden or forgotten, ultimately. In many ways the reciprocity that seems to be returned by outer people and events is actually coming from our true nature, helping us to understand that we are not fundamentally separate from apparent others. As we treat them, we treat ourselves. The Golden Rule illumines multiple dimensions like a holographic beacon.

Less Pride, More Humility

Healthy relationships are a product of healthy emotional states, and these reinforce each other. One of the primary challenges we face in relationships is the underlying indoctrination of the herding culture, which tends to project and encourage unhealthy emotional patterns and responses through all our cultural institutions. We can approach this, for example, through the lens of traditional

Christian practice, and the teaching of the Seven Deadly Sins and the Seven Heavenly Virtues. The first and most harmful of these seven sins is pride. The other six are greed, lust, envy, gluttony, anger, and sloth.

The month of June has been designated Pride Month by the U.S. government, and it goes without saying that it is essential that our gay brothers and sisters be fully included and protected in our society, and that the pride movement has been helpful in raising awareness about the issue of gay rights. Nevertheless, words have power, and extolling pride as a virtue to be celebrated seems problematic in the bigger picture of our relationships. Our compassion can be weaponized against us to serve the nefarious agendas of the plutocrats who control governments, medical, and media narratives. It behooves us to make diligent efforts to understand what is actually going on behind the deceptive facades erected on pretexts of caring.

These agendas are carefully designed, and using the pretext of caring about others, the ruling oligarchs inundate us with messages promoting pride, such as being proud of being gay, and proud of being overweight, and so forth. What is pride, exactly? In terms of psychological and spiritual health, it is one of the most harmful poisons, and yet it is celebrated as a virtue. A hallmark of sociopathic tyrannical forces is the tactic of reversal, of turning things on their head in order to confuse and dominate others. The more we can be corrupted to abandon spiritual values such as humility, integrity, and self-reliance, the more easily we can be controlled. It is foundational to all spiritual teachings that we make an effort to purify our actions by reducing egocentricity and cultivating genuine kindness for others, summed in the universal teaching of The Golden Rule.

The teaching of the Seven Deadly Sins aligns with this, but in mainstream media narratives this teaching is reversed and the harmful emotional states are encouraged, and the more noble and virtuous ones are mocked. The way things are going, perhaps before long we'll have a Gluttony Month, a Greed Month, and a Sloth Month as well because these poisons, like pride and all the rest, are relentlessly promoted. Why? They boost profits and weaken us socially, ethically, and psychologically so that we are more easily exploited and controlled.

Exploring these seven poisons and their brazen promotion by the wealthy ruling class, we continue with the first one, pride. What is it about pride that makes it particularly harmful? For one thing, it makes us unteachable. With pride, we close our minds and hearts. We are typically conditioned from childhood to be proud of being recognized for our accomplishments, but this tends to disconnect us from genuine self-respect that is not based on pleasing others. Pride also promotes a tendency in us to discount or disconnect from the harm we cause others. We are all born and raised in a culture that imprisons, sexually abuses, and kills millions of animals on a daily basis, and the underlying legitimization for this toxic violence is that we are superior to animals and nature, so we can own them and do with them whatever we like. We are superior and they are inferior, says the narrative in which we are embedded from birth. Their suffering at our hands is deemed inconsequential. We can ask cows, pigs, chickens, and other animals what they think about human pride and how it affects our relationship with them. There is no more destructive force in our world or our relationships than pride, and yet our culture celebrates it in an ongoing orgy of wasting animals, ecosystems, and each other.

This is one of the hidden furies driving our diseases, wars, and unhappiness. Pride goeth before a fall, for a reason. If we study the ancient Greek tragedies, where the tragic hero always suffers a fall, we see that it is due to his own character defects, which are mainly two: hubris and obtuseness. Hubris is the overweening pride that distorts perception, and leads to obtuseness, the inability to understand the truth of a situation. We see it today playing out as catastrophic gullibility, with many of us complying with, and failing to question, the medical, political, and food agendas that turn us from sovereign and creative individuals into consumers, and into mere livestock to be exploited.

The same is true of the other deadly sins. All are promoted and celebrated in our corporate-driven media and culture, to the detriment of our relationships, health, and freedom. Looking at the second one, greed, it is obvious that those who are the most honored and respected in our society are those with the most greed. It is those with extreme wealth whose wasteful consumerist lives are not only emulated, but who have been able to turn their wealth into power, and who control not just our governments but every institution in our culture, for their own benefit. The agendas being promoted by these plutocrats through their organizations, such as the World Economic

Forum, the Council on Foreign Relations, the United Nations, the World Health Organization, the Bilderberg Group, and the Trilateral Commission, concentrate and centralize power in the hands of a few. If allowed to continue unchecked, this rule by the greediest among us will reflect the same tyranny which we relentlessly inflict on animals we view as livestock. The entire foundation of our society—consumerism—is based on greed, and the destructive delusion that consumerist greed will bring us happiness, and that those who consume the most conspicuously are worthy to enjoy the highest status.

The third deadly sin is lust. We have billion-dollar industries promoting adornments, beauty products, fashions, films, music, and other products that promote harmful lust in our population. Sex is used to sell virtually everything, from cars and tools to clothes and food. Women are sexualized as objects to be used, and it is getting so extremely perverse now that even children are being sexualized. Lust turns beings into things. The lust for flesh turns cows into burgers, and turns other human beings into objects to be used for one's own pleasure and gain. This is a sure foundation for unhealthy and exploitive relationships, and suffering and misery as well.

The fourth and fifth deadly sins are envy and gluttony, and it is obvious that our society celebrates and promotes these as well. Envy is weaponized as a force and used in advertising to boost profits by propelling us to buy more, consume more, and to continually compare ourselves to others, and compete with them not just in amount and quality of our possessions, but in the image—the mask—that we project into the world. The addictive yearning for approval from others to validate our self-worth drives insatiable envy, a destructive poison to healthy relationships. In a similar way, gluttony has perversely become a virtue in our consumerist culture, and consuming to excess is seen as a mark of success, and as a right that can never be questioned or criticized. We have armies of scientists working to create addictive flavors and textures in food to compel us to overeat, and similar legions of advertising companies urging us to be proud of our overconsumption and of our obesity. With gluttony, we not only exploit; we are also exploited.

The final two vices, anger and sloth, are also blatantly promoted in our society, and are reinforced by the other five. Anger is an energy of exclusion and reinforces our sense of separateness from others, and is also, like all of these poisons, harmful to our overall physical and psychological health, as well as our relationships. We are encouraged to cultivate anger against enemy nations and leaders, and against those we are told are dangerous and other, such as those of different political views or vaccine status, and we are encouraged to censor and cancel them. Identity politics thrives on self-righteous anger, and on the culturally-promoted notion that we have the right to be righteously offended by what other people say or do. This is the opposite of cultivating understanding, respect, patience, and awareness, and feeds right into the globalist agenda of the few dominating the many by dividing us and promoting conflicts within society.

The entirety of our technological culture is based on encouraging sloth, with the primary appeal of scientific orthodoxy being that we can be more comfortable and secure and save work by using all kinds of machines and devices that allow us do more sitting, relaxing, and self-indulgent consuming. President John Kennedy appealed to citizens back in the early 1960s to cultivate vigor and decried what he saw as a terrible encroaching softness in the American people, challenging everyone to get in sufficient shape to be able to successfully complete a 50-mile march. In the sixty intervening years, our sloth and obesity have both increased dramatically, unfortunately, and it is not just physical sloth, but more insidiously, intellectual laziness as well. This manifests as the devastating gullibility that is rampant in our world today, with vast swathes of our population blindly accepting, without vigorously questioning, whatever narratives and mandates are proclaimed by the technocratic establishment. Even if it means unparalleled losses of freedom, wellness, and basic human rights, we find there is a well-cultivated inability to make the necessary efforts needed to protect our human dignity and sovereignty, and assure them for our children.

These seven emotional afflictions are deadly to the health of all relationships and to our health, and it's essential to understand how and why they are propagated in our society so that we can protect ourselves and counteract their harmful influence. We are called to proactively counteract these dark forces with our full awareness, and to recognize them clearly when they assert themselves in our thoughts and feelings. Naming them, seeing them, and unmasking them takes away their power. These harmful vices often hide behind deceptive facades that trick us into embracing them.

The antidote is to evoke and practice the wisdom of The Golden Rule, and do our best to nurture, within our actions, speech, and thoughts, the Seven Heavenly Virtues. These help to raise our consciousness to a higher level where the Seven Deadly Sins, which are reinforced perpetually by media messaging and our cultural programming, are less able to influence and corrupt us. As part of this, we stop consuming mainstream films, television and radio, as well as corporate print and online media, and other toxic media, and reconnect with our discernment and inner discriminating awareness wisdom.

The seven virtues, corresponding to and liberating us from the seven sins, are humility, charity, chastity, gratitude, temperance, patience, and diligence. Humility opens our heart to the beauty of others and of nature, and to an abiding sense of respect for all expressions of life. We realize that we can learn, grow, and improve the quality of our consciousness by making genuine efforts, and this can gradually liberate us from the miserable prison of pride. Likewise, practicing charity and generosity naturally heals the tendencies toward greed, opening our heart to the joy of helping others without expecting a return. Chastity liberates us from the cultural indoctrination that conditions us to narrow our view of ourselves and others to satisfy cravings that are constantly being stimulated by the media. We learn to establish our consciousness at the level where we recognize and value others as complete beings worthy of respect and kindness. Gratitude is pure gold, dissolving the corrosive delusion of desiring what others have, and the misery of comparing and judging. Cultivating gratitude, we appreciate the countless small beauties that surround us, and develop our capacity to savor the immense richness, abundance, and potentialities of our brief and precious human life. Instead of envying others, we savor and celebrate their successes, health, and good fortune.

Patience arises out of compassion and understanding, dissolving anger, frustration, and ill-will, and bringing peace and harmony into our mind and into our relationships with others. Practicing temperance, we realize that consuming outer experiences never brings fulfillment, and as we free ourselves from the yearning to impress and accumulate, temperance naturally arises in us, without effort. It is nothing to be proud of. With awareness, we no more desire to over-consume harmful drink, food, or other substances and experiences than we would desire to put our hand on a hot stove burner. We see clearly it is doing nothing but causing unnecessary suffering to ourselves and others. Finally, diligence is the outer manifestation of connecting with our spiritual purpose in this lifetime. There is no virtue more important than diligence. With it, our progress is absolutely guaranteed, and without it, little progress will ever be possible.

As we reconnect, through practicing these virtues, with the unique mission that is ours to fulfill during this valuable time on Earth, we are naturally filled with enthusiasm and vitality. We are inspired to do our best to unfold our potentialities so that we can contribute our particular melody to the great song of awakening and healing that is growing and singing within the heart of humanity.

These spiritual practices of cultivating the healthy qualities that open doorways to beneficial and fulfilling relationships, and firmly rejecting the unhealthy attitudes that cause addiction, misery, and unnecessary suffering, are not unique to Christianity. Virtually all religions and spiritual traditions emphasize the importance of this type of purification practice. This is one reason religious teachings and traditions are despised by globalist pluto-crats and technocrats, who seek to dominate and exploit humanity. Upstanding, ethical, spiritually-aware people are vastly more difficult to subdue than self-centered, amoral, and materialistic people are.

As another example, there is the recognition in the Buddhist tradition that our minds are harmed by what are referred to as the Five Poisons: ignorance, anger, greed, pride, and envy. The effort is made, through right living, mindfulness, and meditation, to transform these Five Poisons into the Five Wisdoms. Ignorance is transformed into the Wisdom of All-Encompassing Space, anger into the Great Mirror Wisdom, greed into the Discriminating Awareness Wisdom, pride into the Wisdom of Equanimity, and envy into the Wisdom of All-Accomplishing Action. As in the Christian practice of the transformation of the seven poisonous delusions into the seven virtues, the emphasis is on continuous and diligent practice in every-day life. Both vegan living and spirituality are cultivated and developed through dedicated effort, and this effort is, ultimately, its own reward, raising our understanding and the quality of our consciousness, health, and relation-ships, and increasing our capacity to contribute to our culture.

While we may not have control over the actions of others and of society itself, we always have control over the quality of our responses to these actions. This is indeed an enormously liberating and transformational power. Cultivating patience, gratitude, generosity, and doing our best to inquire deeply into our true nature, we can sow seeds that reclaim healthy relationships with others, supporting freedom and harmony in our world.

All Our Relations

There is significant healing power in our human touch, which we can give and receive. There is the illustrative story of Kyrie and Brielle Jackson, twin girls who were born prematurely and were only about two pounds. They were placed in separate incubators at the hospital to prevent infection, and while Kyrie started to stabilize and get stronger, Brielle was fading away toward dying. The attending nurse broke protocol and put Brielle in with Kyrie, and she snuggled up to Kyrie, who put her arm around her and within minutes Brielle's breathing and heart-rate stabilized and her temperature rose to normal, and her life was saved.[74] This is referred to as a rescue hug, and it is good to be aware that when we are touched by someone we trust, it sets off a healing process whereby the skin proprioceptors send a message to the vagus nerve which lowers blood pressure and heart rate, and reduces stress hormones like cortisol. Cortisol is the fight-or-flight hormone that, if chronically present due to unalleviated stress, decreases immune functions, suppresses thyroid function, raises blood pressure, decreases bone and muscle density, creates blood sugar imbalances, and increases abdominal fat, among other things. We can provide and receive loving touch in trust situations, and this includes even with companion animals, and to a lesser extent self-touch. People all around us need rescue hugs and loving touch, and it can be physically, or with a smile, a kind word, or a virtual message. The more we activate our consciousness as healers, the healthier our world becomes.

All of our relationships are interconnected, and looking deeply, we see that we are always relating, in the sense that we are ever participating with the world around us. The way we do anything is, most likely, the way we do everything. Our outer actions, words, gestures, and style of being reflect our inner consciousness. If we understand how we are all related, we realize that we relate not just to the people in our lives, but to every being, object, and situation with which we interact. For example, the way we hang up the kitchen dishtowel reflects our awareness, as does the way we put away our clothes, and everything else, and our actions affect us and radiate into the infinitely interconnected web of relations. If we pay attention to the dishtowel, and are loving in our relationship with the dishtowel, we create the foundation for feeling loved, because when we are loving we also feel loved. We can practice being loving throughout our entire day, without having to run out and find a mate through a dating site, simply going through our day. Whatever we sow in our small-scale actions, we inevitably reap on a larger scale, as the reciprocal interest on our actions compounds over time.

This practice of treating even household objects with respect and kindness deepens the foundation of our attitudes so that we tend to be loving with other people, with

animals, with situations, and with ourselves. It is especially helpful to practice kindness toward small defenseless animals such as insects, and do our best to refrain
from harming them unnecessarily. We are raised in a
society where we are taught to look at small beings like
insects as pests, and we use poisons to attack and destroy
them by the millions. If instead we do our best to practice
patience, to relocate or discourage them with herbs or
non-toxic methods, and to communicate and treat insects
with respect, we sow seeds for harmony in all our relations. It is but a step from viewing insects as pests to be
eliminated, to viewing human beings as pests to be eliminated. We can always practice treating others with kindness, and we can take this practice of lovingkindness right
down to the kitchen sink level, and even to our shoes, our
gestures, and each breath that we receive and give out
into the world. The more we let go of seeing and treating
others as objects—even physical objects themselves—and
view and treat them instead as sacred manifestations of
the infinite love that is the source of all, the more we find
harmony, love, and grace flowering as living forces in our
awareness.

Taking responsibility for the quality of our consciousness, as well as the quality of our relationships and
the quality of our physical health, we see how we are all
interconnected. The primary impediment to healthy and
harmonious relationships is our clinging to the self-concept
that we have built up, which puts our interests first, and
makes a continual effort to project a particular image to the
world. This sense of separateness leads to a whole pano-
ply of vices, conflicts, and suffering, and blocks the healing

power of humility, purity, and love. Fifteenth-century Zen master Ikkyu said, "He who answers when called is nothing but a thief." The thief referred to here is our acculturated sense of self, and instead of identifying with the little thief of our separate self, we can make an effort to inquire into and eventually discover our original face: our face before we were born and before our parents were born. This is the original face whose source we all share, and which we can honor, respect, and enjoy as we discover it in ourselves and see it in others.

Realizing that we are essentially eternal consciousness, which makes the apparent self possible, we expand our heart to include others as equal, sovereign, and magnificent expressions. The resurrecting power of love flows more and more freely and fully through our mind and heart. We can wink to each other as we go through life (and to animals, trees, and insects as well), savoring our uniqueness, understanding our essential unity, and always including all living beings within the circle of our kindness and respect. Love is the primary healing power, and doing our inner work opens us to be vehicles for this in all our relationships.

Brother Fly

Emerging from morning meditation. . .
Smooth sweet flow of mind. . .
Resting, beyond thoughts, quiet. . .
Eyes opening slowly. . . and captivated!
A miracle joins me on the bedspread!
A beautiful little fly, quietly sitting,
Occasionally rubbing front legs together,
And now and then his back legs.
Suddenly I love this precious fly so strongly!
As if in response, he turns, facing me directly,
And stops all moving, poised and quiet.
I admire his delicacy, ability, perfection;
The moment stretches, swallowing time. . .
We are brothers, I feel it,
Created by the same mysterious Hand.
He flies to my shoulder; I feel blessed.
There is a communion in this room,
A sacred moment of understanding.
We are safe in each other's presence, and free.
Infinite Love fills every space in the universe.

Chapter Four

THE FOURTH KEY: THE HEALING POWER OF MOVEMENT

"The wound is the place where the Light enters you."
—RUMI

"Our growing softness, our increasing lack of physical fitness, is a menace to our security."
—JOHN F. KENNEDY

"The only person you are destined to become is the person you decide to be."
—RALPH WALDO EMERSON

Reconnecting with Natural Movement and Posture
Another of the essential keys to radiant health is movement and exercise. Our body is made to move, and we live in a culture that in many ways thwarts our natural

impulses for authentic movement from infancy onward. Fortunately, we can make an effort to learn, practice, and engage in healthy modes of moving, reclaiming harmony for our body and mind, and connecting with nature and with our original undivided nature.

It is instructive that Dr. Brian Clement, the director of Hippocrates Wellness Institute in Florida, who has supervised the successful treatment of tens of thousands of people through an organic vegan (mainly raw) diet and an overall holistic approach, emphasizes that the three primary keys to radiant health are nutrition, exercise, and attitude, with special emphasis on attitude. We have been discussing nutrition and attitude throughout this book, especially in the immediately preceding sections on nutrition, meditation, and relationships, and now as we explore the importance of movement and exercise, we begin with a reminder that this is also a vast area of inquiry and exploration. We are simply providing a broad-brush treatment in this section.

There are two main areas to address when it comes to movement. One is inquiring into the way our bodies are moving throughout the day, and how we have been conditioned to carry and use our bodies. The other is delving into the broad arena of movement practices, such as athletics, yoga, tai chi, and the many modalities we can engage to increase our endurance, strength, balance, flexibility, and the general health of our body through physical exercises of various kinds. Both are fascinating explorations that could easily occupy many lifetimes (and libraries) of research and experience.

I have found it helpful to realize how our culture's essential orientation toward animals and nature, which is one of superiority, and a general sense of uneasiness and separation regarding them, negatively affects our health not just through the harmful animal-based and chemically-toxified foods and products that we are eating and using, but also through our whole bodily experience on Earth.

"Get up from the ground!" The city harlot shouts this at Enkidu, in the ancient Sumerian *Epic of Gilgamesh*, arguably the oldest extant story of our species, written almost 4,000 years ago. Enkidu, who up until this time is at ease in nature, and runs and consorts with all the wild animals, who are his friends, rises up from his sitting position on the Earth and leaves his amiable wilderness and travels with her to Uruk, "the city of the strong walls." He lives in the city and is so changed by the experience, that when he again visits the forest, all the animals run away from him. This represents the ancient cultural transition to herderism with its ownership of animals and nature, from which we still suffer today. Our imperious alienation from the Earth is more severe than ever, and is articulated not just in our meals, but in our architecture, furnishings, and technology as well. We live and move within constructed boxes detached from nature, and we sit in chairs for long periods, and prop ourselves up on couches. As a result, our muscles, joints, and tendons are disconnected from their natural flexibility and strength.

When I left home right after college in 1975 with my brother Ed, walking south on our spiritual pilgrimage eventually to Alabama from Massachusetts, I was enthusiastic to question my social indoctrination, and to learn from the wisdom of other cultures, especially Eastern cultures. I believed this would assist me in making progress in what was the most important thing, meditation practice. We slept on the ground in the forest or on the floor of churches most nights (the rare beds were usually in harrowing situations like small-town jails or rescue missions). I began to relish being close to the Earth for sleeping, and for meditating. But sitting on the ground was painful because, like Ed, I had played a lot of ice hockey and had a case of "hockey legs," with hard, tight muscles that made it hard to flatten my knees toward the Earth when sitting cross-legged on the ground. Nevertheless, the idea of being able to sit comfortably and upright on the Earth and meditate for long periods of time intrigued me. I kept at it, and as the days and weeks went by, my legs and body relaxed and the tight muscles loosened to the point that when we eventually arrived in Huntsville and discovered the Zen Center there, it was possible to sit for many hours on the floor in meditation.

The Zen community there was welcoming, and we were given our own room where we could live and meditate as much as we liked, on our own. Meditation and yoga classes were held in the evenings and so we sat in meditation during the day for eight hours, practiced an hour of yoga daily to become more flexible, and then attended the evening classes. Since then, I have never used the usual western furniture, except when sitting in restaurants, and so forth, because I discovered the perfect alternative: zafus and zabutons. A few months after we arrived at the Zen center, I attended my first (and not my last) zafu- and zabuton-making party. We all helped to sew and stuff about 30 zabutons and zafus. The former are cotton batting-filled mats roughly three feet square, and the latter are round kapok-filled cushions about a foot in diameter. These two basic oriental Zen furnishings are all I have used for the past fifty years. Madeleine loves them also, and in our RV and our home in northern California, I sit at a home-made low table to work at the computer on a zafu and zabuton, and we eat meals on zafus at our low dining room table, or outside on the deck with our plates on our laps.

I feel enormously blessed to be somewhat liberated from standard Western furniture, and more importantly, to at least be aware of the mentality that created it. It is well understood that to be able to enter deeper states of meditation, it's important that our body be erect, with a straight, self-supporting spine. It helps to have our hips tilted forward, shoulders back, head relaxed and balanced, naturally at ease, poised, and in harmony. Sitting on the Earth or floor on a small cushion with the legs folded in the full lotus or half lotus position is ideal for this, and naturally tends to bring our mind into a sense of alert and calm awareness. Standing up from the floor and sitting down again are natural ways to increase strength and flexibility in muscles and joints, and are a gentle form of exercise in which people naturally engaged many dozens of times daily in earlier times. Sitting in typical chairs is the opposite of all this. The body is folded in an unnatural way, with the back being supported, hips tilted backward, lower back curving, pulling the shoulders forward, with the upper back slumping. The head projects forward, creating physical and mental stress and reducing both circulation and clarity. As kids we are compelled to sit still in these harmful devices by well-meaning adults who were similarly abused as children.

The solution of course is to make an effort to find or create alternatives, and this is gradually happening as more people adopt desks that allow them to stand, and even to walk, while working, and alternative types of support that encourage spinal health like kneeling chairs, floor cushions, inflatable balls, cushioned floor benches, and so forth. With practice, we can strengthen and increase the flexibility of our muscles and joints, and even learn to adopt the ancient and universal posture of squatting, which is still popular among millions of people in less industrialized countries.

When I was a Zen monk in Korea, one of the liberating discoveries I made was the vast superiority of the squatting position for defecating. It is, again, quite a tragedy how we are taught as children to sit on a toilet seat with our legs dangling down, which puts our colon in a disadvantageous position for eliminating waste. The universal position for thousands of years has been the squat, both for defecating and for giving birth, but these empowering and natural positions have been taken away from us, and we suffer as a result. Few people are even aware of this, because nobody talks about it. Back in the 1980s, traveling around Korea, virtually all of the toilets were in the floor and everyone squatted over them, except for a few facilities in public places like train stations that had one stall with a sit-down type toilet, marked, "For Westerner." Returning to Korea 30 years later, I found there were few of the traditional squat toilets left. Along with a sharp increase in Western customs of meat and dairy consumption, Western-style toilets have helped increase pharmaceutical profits on a global scale as constipation and colon diseases proliferate. Fortunately, by simply placing a small foot stool in front of a toilet, it is easy to approximate the traditional squatting position. Regular elimination is an essential foundation of health, and a fiber-rich whole-food, plant-sourced diet is an excellent foundation for this. Many years ago, I heard the celebrated Buddhist scholar John Blofeld at a lecture tell the audience that he eliminated his bowels every morning right after rising, by squatting (he lived in Thailand) and gently massaging his abdomen in a clockwise direction. This healthy regime works remarkably well, but we rarely hear about it.

The main point of this first section on movement is to encourage us all to explore alternatives to the ways we have been taught to walk, sit, move, and be in our herding culture, and to reconnect with more natural, playful, earth-oriented ways of moving and being. As another example, it's fascinating to explore our culture's footwear and how it interferes with our natural bodily wisdom and vitality. One obvious example of course is the custom of adding heels of various lengths to shoes. The higher they are, the more they wreak havoc with healthy posture, balance, stability, and connectedness with the Earth. Through energy meridians, as well as through our circulatory, lymphatic, and nervous systems, our feet are more connected than we often realize with the rest of our body and with our mental state. Footwear often harmfully constricts the bones, ligaments, and flow of blood and energy in our feet, causing other problems that may seem unrelated.

As the book *Born to Run* documents, walking and running barefoot is ideal for us because it naturally strengthens the tendons, ligaments, and muscles in our feet, ankles, and legs, and properly aligns our spine so that we are running and walking in ways for which we are designed, which energizes our body, contributes to proper posture and overall good health. Over the years, running shoes have added more and more padding to the soles, encouraging us to land on our heels when running, rather than on our toes or mid-foot as we do when barefoot, leading to the common complaint among runners of back pain and knee problems. Fortunately, some shoe companies[75] provide footwear with remarkably thin soles, so that it is almost like walking barefoot, while still providing a modicum of protection and decorum.

Another aspect is that the soles of virtually all footwear are now made of rubber, and thus act as insulators from the Earth's vibratory field. We spend most of our time in houses and cars, and walk with rubber-soled shoes, and may thus be almost completely disconnected from the Earth's energy field. Many people have found that the practice of "earthing"—consciously bringing the soles of our feet into direct contact with the grass, soil, rocks, and water of the Earth, and sitting on and lying on the Earth without the interference of rubber or plastic mats or carpets—brings healing to both chronic and acute conditions previously unresponsive to medical treatments.[76]

In sum, it is essential to do our best to become aware of our bodies and practice mindful movement throughout the day, realizing that many of the props that are taken for granted and normalized in our living spaces, such as chairs, desks, automobiles, furnishings, shoes, clothing, floors, walls, and ceilings have all conditioned us, often from infancy, to habitually move and hold our bodies in ways that contribute to stress and disease. We can experiment, learn from other cultures, and discover and practice new ways of moving and being that build health, joy, resilience, creativity, and freedom into our lives. For example, yawning and stretching are well-recognized ways that our bodies release tension, oxygenate, and invigorate themselves (and us), and yet we often feel inhibited and repress these healthy urges. Right now, you can stop reading for a moment and engage a big, full-bodied yawn and stretch, and feel the difference it makes. Regular yawning is connected with oxygenation of our tissues, better circulation and concentration, and is one of the keys to healthy vision as well. Like everything we have been discussing in this book, we are called to be willing to question and quite often go against social norms and customs to reclaim our health, vitality, awareness, and freedom.

Movement and Exercise

The second area we can explore in this section on healthy and mindful movement is an overview of the many possibilities available to us to engage in exercises and bodily practices that are beneficial. The basic principle is simple: the human body loves to move and thrives on movement.

Sitting still in meditation can bring inner peace, clarity, and wisdom. We can also meditate while running, walking, washing the dishes, and moving throughout our day. The attitude of mindful awareness adds another dimension and can bring a sense of grace and harmony to everything we are doing. Our life is, in many ways, a series of gestures. The more we can bring our daily gestures into alignment with our values and with the inner song of our being, the more we find that we are living our life as a meaningful and creative adventure.

Several movement traditions from Asia have profound wisdom embedded within them. We could study them for many lifetimes without exhausting all their benefits. From India, for example, we have the practice of many types of yoga, such as pranayama, which is working with primordial energy (prana) through breathing practices. Another type is hatha (literally sun/moon) yoga, which is what most people in the West think of as yoga, because it has to do with cultivating the ability to maintain a wide variety of postures (asanas) that increase our body's strength, flexibility, and balance. There are many schools and traditions within hatha yoga, each with its unique emphases and contributions, with some being more rigorous, some more flowing, some more gentle, or more acrobatic, or meditative. The origins of hatha yoga stretch back into prehistoric antiquity. One of the narratives explaining its origins is that yogis found that their bodies would spontaneously adopt certain positions with specific inner meditative states, and that teaching these positions and postures to their students would help the students find their way to these elevated mental states.

Like with any physical discipline, the key to reaping benefits is proper and regular practice, and clarity about the purpose of practicing. The hatha yogic tradition, as part of the larger Indian yogic tradition, aims to help the practitioner attain a more unified and spiritualized consciousness. Practicing the postures—and there are hundreds of them—definitely helps us to develop strength, flexibility, and balance. There is a danger with yoga also, as with most physical exercises, of pushing too hard and injuring the body, and an awareness of this is important as we practice, to be sure not to attempt to stretch too far when the body is cold, for example. Regular and proper practice of yoga brings many health benefits, and this accounts for its rapidly increasing popularity. These benefits include not just muscle tone, poise, and flexibility, but also the stimulation of life-force energy (prana) flowing through the channels of the body.

Cultivating Energy for Vitality and Healing

According to the ancient yogic tradition there are many subtle energy channels (*nadis*) in the body, and three primary ones, which are the *sushumna* (central channel going up the spine) and the *ida* and *pingala,* the left and right channels, which weave back and forth around the central channel, like two ascending serpents. This energy, coiled at the base of the spine, is said to be awakened by meditation, yoga, and spiritual practice. It begins to rise from the lowest energy center, or *chakra,* the *muladhara*, up through these primary nadis, eventually to the crown of the head, which is the seventh energy center, the *sahasrara chakra*. This movement of *pranic* life-energy, also called *kundalini,* from the base of the spine up to the crown, is connected with the spiritual journey that transforms material survival-based consciousness to the transcendent and liberated consciousness abiding as our true nature. According to some traditions, this image of two serpents rising up a staff is the ancient origin of the caduceus that is still used as a symbol of medicine, which originally, before the ascension of allopathy, emphasized holistic healing arts based on spiritually elevating human consciousness.

Some yogas work with this rising kundalini energy, which stimulates seven energy centers that correspond to states of consciousness that become more refined with each ascending chakra. From the first chakra, the *muladhara,* the seat of basic survival drives at the base of the spine, it rises to the second, the *svathisthana,* residing in the lower abdomen area of the genitals, representing procreation and family life, to the third, the *manipura* in the solar plexus region, representing power and accomplishment, to the fourth, the *anahatta* in the heart area, representing altruistic love for others, to the fifth, the *vissudha* in the throat, representing inspired creative expression, to the sixth, the *ajna* chakra in the center of the forehead, representing intuitive insight and inner wisdom, to the seventh, the *sahasrara,* representing the full flowering of the human potential as unbounded consciousness aware of its essential unity with the source of all life. As long as we are living our life primarily from the three lower energy centers, motivated by fear and survival concerns, by sensual desire, and by ambition for power, status, and prestige, we find that our mind is often agitated, our emotions conflicted, and our body is typically in a state of disharmony and stress, manifesting various symptoms as it attempts to cleanse the mental and physical toxins with which it is besieged.

When our consciousness rises, we begin to question the cultural indoctrination of materialism, and live more in the upper chakras of lovingkindness, inspiration, and creativity. Following our inner guidance and opening to higher aspirations of cooperation, generosity, and harmony with the source of our life, we find that our experience of vitality and radiant health naturally expands as our vibratory level rises. We tend to release fears of all kinds as we increasingly realize that we are serving a higher understanding of life, and that our purpose is to be contagious as we spread healing, freedom, humor, kindness, and joy into the interdependent web of relations that connects all expressions of life. The haloes that artists have employed to convey the spiritual light that radiates from sages, saints, and mystics from all times and regions reflect this basic understanding that as we activate and dwell within the higher energy centers, our being shines forth an illuminating and healing presence into the world.

This sheds light on the spiritual vision that underlies the practice of the various yoga postures and movements. When we adopt higher motivations in our practice of yoga (and in our practice of daily life as well), we not only bring more strength, balance, and flexibility to our muscles, ligaments, bones, and tendons, but also stimulate the latent energy currents which, though unrecognized by western medicine, can bring strength, balance, and flexibility to our consciousness as well. This helps to build our immunity to the lower vibrational distractions and impediments of the human world. Ultimately, just as yoga means union, we realize that every action, movement, and gesture that we make throughout the day is our practice of yoga, and that by cultivating breath awareness and bringing mindfulness to our activities, we are healing old wounds of self-centeredness and anxiety, and uniting with the healing power of awareness. Our English words heal, health, and healing come from the old root word *hale*, meaning whole, and reflect this ancient understanding that genuine healing arises in our body-mind as we become whole through our realization of deeper truths.

While it is helpful to be aware of the many benefits in the healing and wisdom traditions that precede and, in many ways, transcend the materialistic medical model in which we have been raised, it is important to remember that there are potential dangers as well, if our motivation, understanding and practice are not in alignment with deeper realities. Just as we can impatiently push our tendons too hard and strain them, we can also push too hard with pranayama and other practices, and awaken more kundalini energy than we are yet able to handle, so it is best to have a qualified teacher when exploring further into these potent realms of mind-body healing.

Yoga emerged in ancient times in India, and with it, a profound system of healing, known as ayurveda, also arose. In China, the age-old practices of chi gong and tai chi developed as somewhat comparable traditions. Like yoga, they are based on bodily movements, poses, and cultivating energy in channels, both in and around the spine, and also in what are referred to as the twelve acupuncture meridians, foundational to the ancient system of healing known as acupuncture, as well as acupressure and moxibustion. Yoga is based on understanding and cultivating prana, and similarly, chi gong (spelled qigong is the new Pinyin system) and tai chi call this universal life energy *chi*. Qigong tends to focus on postures and slow repetitive movements that aim to generate and build up the quality and quantity of chi energy in our body, while tai chi is comprised of more complex slow-motion movements that are strung together in long sequences to cultivate the ability to move chi energy through the body. Both are related to healing, and the cultivation of energy that can be used for healing ourselves and others, and they are also foundational to the broad spectrum of Asian martial arts practices such as aikido, taekwondo, judo, karate, kung fu, and so forth.

Though I don't consider myself an expert by any means, I have been practicing yoga, tai chi, and qigong for forty years now, and find all three to be exceptionally valuable allies in living a healthy and harmonious life. They are all different, but complement each other. Qigong and tai chi are rooted in ancient Taoist philosophy, which emphasizes harmony with nature and the practice of meditation, and also includes practices that raise the chi from the base of the spine up to the crown of the head. Interestingly, in Taoist energy practice, once the chi rises up the spine and reaches the crown of the head, the practitioner then continues on and allows the energy to flow down the front of the body back to the base reservoir in the abdomen, completing the orbit and making a circuit of the energy. I find this to be an intriguing insight into these two powerful cultures and their overall orientations. Indian philosophy and spirituality are marked with tremendous ascending fervor, flowery and abstruse intricacies, and a sense of propulsion beyond this world. Chinese philosophy and spirituality reflect a sense of being grounded, simple, matter-of-fact, sublimely subtle, understated, and very much related to this Earth and living in this world. Both offer remarkable potentials for liberation, healing, and insight, and both are based on complex, nuanced cosmologies stretching far back into prehistory.

In China, for example, there is the underlying idea of wu chi, the primordial non-dual being that is symbolized by an empty circle, from which manifests the tai chi, which is the familiar yin/yang symbol of black flowing into white and vice-versa, with each containing a small dot of its complementary opposite. From these primordial yang (heaven/bright/expansive/creative) and yin (earth/dark/contractive/receptive) energies are born their ever-increasingly complex combinations that we see manifested all around us in nature and within us, and in the situations of our worldly life, represented by the eight trigrams and 64 hexagrams of the *I Ching*, an ancient text still widely used to help reveal the subtle energetic patterns in the ever-changing specific conditions in which we find our lives unfolding. Thus, qigong and tai chi work with not just the explosive force and strength of yang energy, but also with the flowing, yielding, non-resistant water-like power of yin energy, colloquially referred to as "hard" and "soft." There is a poignant wisdom in this, and in understanding how to use movement and exercise for health in ways that are often completely contrary to how we have been conditioned in the West.

Many of the postures and movements of qigong and tai chi are inspired by the ancient practice of closely observing animals in nature, learning to adopt their ways of moving, and imitating their bodily gestures, thereby increasing vitality, health, and longevity. As with yoga, there are countless schools, traditions, and esoteric practices within the world of chi training. A foundational paradox in qigong training is that the slower one moves, the more chi is generated. Many of us find that regular practice of qigong and tai chi brings a sense of grace and immediacy into unavoidable daily life activities—such as washing dishes, sweeping floors, walking, sitting down, and standing up. This can help us appreciate ordinary daily life experiences more fully.

One main principle in qigong and tai chi is to keep our attention and energy low in the body, in the lower *dantian,* the "elixir of life reservoir" that is about two inches below the navel, and throughout the day, to move from this center. This keeps us grounded to the Earth and to the stable center of our being, not just physically, but also spiritually. In the West, we are taught to identify with our face and brain, and to go through life basically in our heads, with our heads and eyes stretched out and leading us when we move. This is all completely unconscious, simply inherited as part of our cultural programming. With practice, we can learn to lower the chi energy from our head to our abdomen, and this in itself can have many healing effects, reducing pressure in our heads and relaxing our body and our way of being in the world, and reconnecting us with the abundance and peace of being at home on the Earth and in our body, not as a disembodied head, but as an embodied expression of awareness.

It is not through reading about these ideas, but by making regular daily efforts to practice them, that we see transformational results, and feel the power and vitality of our original nature reestablishing itself in the seat of our daily body-mind experience. While all three of the traditions—yoga, qigong, and tai chi—are typically practiced slowly, it should be noted that they have also inspired the rapid gymnastics of martial arts with flying kicks, flips, and rolls, as well as acrobatic yogis doing one-handed handstands on cliff edges, all of which require the building up of strength, balance, flexibility and, underlying everything, the capacity to direct mental attention and energy into focused and disciplined awareness.

This life-energy that we take in with the breath, and cultivate through these movement disciplines, is recognized to be both healing and invigorating. I noticed when I began practicing qigong and tai chi that my hands would get so energized that I could play the piano with greater dexterity and fluidity. I learned also that as this energy pours through our hands, we can direct it for healing, both for ourselves by placing our palms, for example, on our eyes if they seem tired, or on or toward the bodies of others if they request healing. Energy simply follows consciousness and ultimately, it is consciousness—and our understanding of our true nature as an expression of consciousness—that is the healing power. Healing may be more accurately understood as revealing the essential harmony of our original nature, and allowing this harmony to reestablish itself. Each one of us can facilitate this, and as we learn to generate, mobilize, and direct the ever-present life force, we can work with this long-known but currently suppressed understanding to benefit our bodies and those around us as well.

Aerobic Exercise

Besides these mindful movement disciplines that work with energy to cultivate balance, vigor, and flexibility, there is also the arena of aerobic exercise, which strengthens our heart and circulatory system as well as our muscles, bones, tendons and ligaments, and if done in clean air, vitalizes our cells with oxygen-rich sustenance, mobilizing the cleansing process and toning all our systems. The primary component of our immune system is our lymphatic system, which is comprised of an extensive network of vessels and nodes that transport white blood cells and the lymphatic fluid that removes toxins from our cells. Because there is no heart-like pump for this system, it is the contractions of our muscles that keep the fluid moving and the system healthy. Aerobic exercise not only energizes and cleanses our tissues; it also tends to promote the release of endorphins, endocannabinoids, dopamine, and other factors that stimulate positive emotions and bolster mental health, as well as oxygenating the brain cells for improved functioning.[77]

The deep and full breathing of aerobic exercise causes us to exhale more carbon dioxide, and this is where most weight-loss occurs. It is remarkable to realize that eighty percent of weight loss is accomplished through eliminating carbon through our outbreaths. All the trees, bushes, and plants around us in nature are built primarily of carbon, which they extract from the surrounding air. Through photosynthesis and inhaling carbon dioxide, they build proteins, lipids, and carbohydrates, thus generating leaves, roots, stems, trunks, flowers, seeds, and fruits, and exhale the precious oxygen that we and other animals inhale. The enormous weight of tall trees doesn't come from sucking matter from the ground, or there would be large holes around trees; it comes from the carbon in atmospheric carbon dioxide, and for us, the reverse is true; our bodies lose excess weight by exhaling it as carbon dioxide. This is why cardio exercise is beneficial to maintaining a healthy body that is light and strong, and also why carbon dioxide is an essential ally for maintaining robust forests, fields, orchards, gardens, and planetary ecosystems. With more trees and plants and thus more atmospheric oxygen, our tissues and blood are more fully oxygenated, and more vibrant and healthier. Exercising in oxygen-rich environments like lush forests is especially beneficial.

There are countless forms of aerobic exercise from which to choose, from brisk walking and jogging to sprinting and high-intensity training, as well as activities like swimming, cycling, rebounding, rope-jumping, treadmill walking/running, exercise-ball bouncing, and calisthenics, as well as sports and games like tennis, basketball, hockey, cross-country skiing, boxing, and soccer, and creative movement like dance, and combinations like dancercise, jazzercise, and exer-striding. This last one, exer-striding, combines brisk walking with rubber-tipped poles that are used with stiff arms to help propel the body forward as in Nordic skiing, turning walking into a full-body exercise, which Madeleine loves and has been doing daily for well over a decade now, with many benefits.[78] We can also increase the cardio and skeletal benefits of walking, jogging, and rebounding by wearing weighted vests and using ankle weights or hand-held weights.

This leads into another important area of beneficial exercise, which is weight training. We can use free weights such as barbells and dumbbells, or machines, springs, elastic cords, and other devices, or the body's weight itself, as with push-ups, pull-ups, sit-ups, squats, and so forth, or isometrics. All these can be beneficial in building muscle mass, burning fat, and strengthening bones. Our bodies thrive on being used and put under stress, and to the degree that we fail to do this, and keep them always relaxed and comfortable, to that degree muscles atrophy, bones deteriorate, and general health degenerates.

Specific Adaptation to Imposed Demand

The key concept in movement and exercise has the acronym SAID: Specific Adaptation to Imposed Demand. When we do pull-ups, we are imposing a demand, and our biceps will make a specific adaptation, which is to get larger and stronger. This holds true for not only all types of exercise, but also for how we are moving and holding ourselves. For example, if we are chronically looking down at our cell phone, the bones and muscles in our neck and back will adapt to this imposed demand, resulting in long-term curvature, stress, and damage. SAID, Specific Adaptation to Imposed Demand, is a valuable key to understanding both physical afflictions as well as solutions to these afflictions.

As we can see, there are multiple dimensions to the many-roomed mansion of health-promoting movement and exercise, and they are all intimately connected with the other aspects that contribute to vibrant health. For example, many powerful weight-lifters and swift runners come to realize eventually that without proper nutrition, their efforts to be healthy through physical training and exercise fail because their arteries are clogged, their microbiome is impaired, and the epithelial cells in their blood vessels are damaged by the foods they are eating. While exercise can help our bodies release toxins, it's important to minimize the intake of these toxins in the first place. They can come from many sources, and contemporary living exposes us to an unprecedented barrage of poisons. These are absorbed not just from food, water, air, clothing, and personal care products, but from EMF fields, and from pharmaceutical medications, especially injections, which go straight into our circulatory system, bypassing all natural defenses.

It is essential that we take responsibility for our health and well-being and proactively protect ourselves not just from these poisons, but also from the censorship and narrative-control that attempt to reduce our awareness of what is actually happening. The medical-industrial complex and the governmental agencies it has captured are motivated to amplify everyone's toxic load, and to do this with plausible deniability, because that is the key not just to guaranteed chronic disease and the resultant profits and power, but also to our decreased ability to effectively research, question, under-stand, educate, organize, and mobilize to put an end to the health-destroying practices that are now normalized in our society. We are called to question—and in many cases to ignore and resist—the accepted, recommended, and mandated so-called health protocols, and to proactively search out healthy and empowering alternatives, and practice them diligently so that we develop proficiency and understanding.

Instead of acquiescing to poisonous medications and dispiriting theories, we can go outside and exercise vigorously in the sunshine and aerate our cells with fresh air, cooperating with our body in eliminating toxins, oxygenating our cells, and boosting our immune system with solar energy and vitamin D. Raising our vibratory level, our physiology naturally comes into harmony with the surrounding microorganisms, and they cooperate with our cells and systems, and benefit them as part of the inherently life-affirming nature of the Source of all being. As an ever-growing chorus of researchers reports, so-called germs do not cause disease, but always work to clean up bodily toxins, and are our allies, cohabitating and cooperating with us, and assisting us and all creatures for countless millennia.[79] The web of life is a mutually-supporting whole, but this understanding is suppressed because it contradicts our culture's core reductionistic materialism, its Germ Theory, and its practice of dominating nature and exploiting animals, and is dangerous to the profits and power of the ruling cartels.

As we cultivate life-energy and keep the subtle channels open and flowing, with our mind and heart savoring and eagerly exploring the creative and beneficial opportunities available to us on this Earth, our health is supported and ensured on every level. This is the most empowering health insurance in which we can invest. It is also precisely what the wealthy ruling class is striving to discourage and eliminate through its various alluring deceptions such as the Great Reset, transhumanism, ongoing pandemic fear-porn, the United Nations Agenda 2030, net-zero carbon emissions, water fluoridation, geoengineering/chemtrail spraying, mandated injections, universal basic income, and central bank digital currencies. Anything that centralizes power in the hands of a few necessarily erodes our individual freedom, and this erodes our health on all five levels—physical, cultural, environmental, psychological, and spiritual—as well.

Thriving in our world today calls for us to be savvy and aware, and to provide our bodies not only with the exercise that we now understand is beneficial in incalculable ways to every organ and system, but also to move mindfully, and adopt postures and positions that support well-being and harmony. The long-lived and healthy people of other cultures developed life-ways that integrated exercise into their lives in a natural way, as they worked in gardens and carried water and wood, and climbed up and down hills.

Because we are born into a much more sedentary culture, it's important to consciously counteract this with a combination of both natural and structured movement and exercise. For example, I typically spend about an hour every morning engaging in yoga, qigong, tai chi, and the Five Tibetan Rites practice,[80] as well as other exercises and calisthenics, including bicycling to the nearby lake and taking a swim, and jumping rope or rebounding. Madeleine has her exercise routine as well. We both spend a couple of hours working in the garden and yard every afternoon, and we joke that the garden is our outdoor gym, with all the lifting, carrying, digging, and so forth that are necessary, and that we enjoy in the fresh air and sunshine. Exercise and movement done in nature bathes our body in sunlight, air, and the Earth's energy field that has sustained us and all life for countless millennia.

Ancient Tree Dream Song

Machines!
Screeching and grinding, buzzing and whining,
You assault us, you assault each other,
You assault the Earth.
We armor ourselves and do your bidding—
We are your soldiers in your war.

Where are the flowing wolves, condors, whales?
Where are the flowing people?
Where are the enchanted forests with ancient eyes alive
and dark?
Where are ears that hear deeper silent songs?

Our ears numbed by you machines,
We slave to feed your massive appetites,
We lay waste our homes
And break the spirit of our land.
You machines, who are our offspring and our gods!

We lay down our lives for you,
And progress with vacant vigor into your gleaming jaws.

In the quiet depths of an old-growth forest,
An ancient grandfather tree,
With enormous roots reaching deep into the earth, and
limbs towering into the light
Breathes in from his brothers and sisters around the
globe
The alarming messages of slaughter and destruction,
The reports of an ever-spreading cancer of machines,
And deep within his heart, the ancient grandfather
knows that it is time,
And turns and rises,
And like a cloud slips out of his majestic green-brown
body:
A mist rising from roots, trunk, and branches,
Covering the entire valley and moving, at night,
Into the world of the machine people.
With a vast prayer for the healing of all flowing
creatures,
The tree spirit bears seeds of an ancient song,
And slips silently into the dreams of the soldiers of
destruction:
Into our fitful nighttime visions,
Into the fretful dreams of our elders and the nightmares
of our children,
And in all these dreams, planting the seeds of a prehis-
toric song—
A song sung only by the marrow of our bones,
And heard only by ears alive to the wild celebration.

The grandfather tree spirit comes tonight planting his
seeds,
Tonight, and every night now he seeds our dreams with
Earth's primordial song,
Sung by the blood in our veins.

Will we hear it and wake and lay down our weapons?
Will we turn our worship from the machines of
destruction?
Will we rejoice once more in the dance?
Will we become flowing people again?

Chapter Five

THE FIFTH KEY: THE HEALING POWER OF NATURE

"The goal of life is living in agreement with nature."
—ZENO

"Heaven is under our feet as well as over our heads."
—HENRY DAVID THOREAU

"There is no Wi-Fi in the forest, but I promise you will find a better connection."
—RALPH SMART

The Practice of Reconnecting with Nature

The fifth key to a healthy and joy-filled life is nature: connecting regularly every day with the beauty and vitality of the natural world. We live in increasingly artificial environments, disconnected from the inspiring power of the

Earth and her misty forests, flowing streams, shimmering lakes, intriguing wildlife, starry skies, fragrant air, and healing sunshine. This disconnectedness is unfavorable for our physical, psychological, and spiritual wellbeing for many reasons. Encased in artificially lit and temperature-controlled structures of unnatural shapes, textures, and colors, our consciousness is conditioned and numbed by man-made forms and the underlying mentality of domination and separateness that created them. The continual hum and roar of traffic, machinery, blowers, and technological systems, the toxic chemicals that tend to pervade indoor spaces, the electromagnetic fields of cell phones and electric grids, the poisonous chemtrails in the skies, the visual monotony and unsightliness, and the ubiquitous straight lines: all disconnect us from the free-flowing healing artistry of the natural world. Spending hours gazing into flat screens and navigating malls, suburbs, and cities, it is easy to become lost in the assumptions and timetables of modern technological living, far removed from the organic cycles and life-giving powers of the natural world.

Researchers are realizing, for example, that our indoor living and the use of chemical sunscreens cause pervasive vitamin D deficiency, leading to a variety of chronic disease conditions. Toxic bug sprays and skin creams are absorbed into all of our organs. Wearing shoes keeps us disconnected from the rejuvenating energy fields that the Earth provides us, and may indirectly induce pain and mental agitation. Artificial lighting pollutes our skies, impeding our view of the stars and increasing insomnia.

Madeleine and I have found it wonderfully helpful to practice connecting with nature, daily if possible.

One of our preferred modes is swimming year-round in lakes, streams, and oceans, and the cold water is exhilarating. If for some reason we cannot swim, we at least take a shower with a cold rinse. Baring our soles to the Earth is a daily practice, as is contemplating the night sky. Communing with forests and with lands that are free from human interference, sharing space with birds, fishes, and other animals, and openly experiencing primary forces such as sun, fresh air, rain, and night dampness can all help to restore our overall sense of wellness. It is not surprising that the Buddha attained spiritual enlightenment sitting at the base of a tree in the forest. Researchers have confirmed that simply viewing natural settings releases endorphins and healing hormones in our bodies. Entering nature—not to dominate or hurry through, but humbly, to receive and commune and inquire—is an ever-available source of inspiration, wisdom, and healing.

One of the serious drawbacks of our technology, besides the relentless noise and toxicity it inflicts in countless ways, is the artificial comfort that it provides. We set a thermostat, and lose our natural capacity to adapt to a range of temperatures. We become prisoners of our fear of discomfort, both physically and psychologically, and are conditioned to view nature not as our friend and inspiring benefactor, but rather as a dangerous opponent against which we have to defend ourselves, and conquer in order to survive. As discussed in *Food for Freedom*, this is an inevitable outcome of ten millennia of animal agriculture and the mentality this mandates. Fortunately, we can question our indoctrination and unlearn and reconnect. Simply leaving our cities, suburbs, and human-created world and heading into nature for an hour or a day or a week is a healthful tonic that feeds, rejuvenates, and balances us immediately.

While still mostly unrecognized by academics and wellness professionals, there are a variety of physical and psychological benefits from what is referred to as forest therapy or nature bathing, based partially on the ancient Japanese practice of Shinrin-Yoku, or "forest bathing." According to the Association of Nature and Forest Therapy, "There are many wonderful health benefits attributed to forest therapy including boosted immune function, improved cardiovascular and respiratory health, attention restoration, and a reduction in stress and depression."[81] Some psychotherapists lead wilderness immersion programs to help heal mental and emotional afflictions of various kinds. I witnessed this first-hand for several years in my youth when I was a camp counselor and would bring inner-city and suburban kids into the wilderness for four-day canoe trips on the Delaware River and hikes on the Appalachian Trail, and could see and feel the spontaneous positive changes in their attitudes and emotions.

By good fortune, I grew up in a nature-loving family and in my youth climbed most of the New England mountains, and have fond memories from my young years of ice skating for miles through light snow on the frozen Concord River, skiing the Headwall at Tuckerman's Ravine, canoeing raging white water rivers, sailing the coast of Maine, learning the arts of wilderness living in summer camps and Boy Scout trainings, and ski mountaineering in the San Juan mountains of Colorado with

Outward Bound. Nature is the unsurpassed teacher, guide, and revealer of divine intelligence, power, and beauty. Over the decades since these early days of connecting with nature, I've found nature to be a reliable and deep wellspring of healing and inspiration. Most of *The World Peace Diet* book was handwritten in nature, under trees and in wilderness areas, opening to inspiration from wildlife and from the Earth herself. Taking time to go into nature is taking time to enter the foundational wholesomeness of being that undergirds all life, and this is, unfortunately, no longer experienced by large swaths of humanity. We seem to be increasingly overwhelmed by urban and technological intrusions.

Through Outward Bound, I got a taste of the potential of solo wilderness experiences, and have repeated that many times over the years, and have explored the benefits of going on vision quests. Though this is typically considered a native American tradition, it is a fundamental wisdom element with which we are all gifted as part of our human heritage: to consciously prepare and purify ourselves, and then walk into the wilderness without food, and fast for a period of time, usually about three to four days. This potentially opens doorways to the wisdom and insight of non-ordinary awareness, which begins to emerge through being alone in nature. We then reenter the bustle of modern life and do our best to integrate the transformative gifts that have been received. We can never put a price on such opportunities that are available to us by the grace of the natural world that supports us constantly, whether we are aware of it or not.

Providing experiences in nature along the lines of vision quests has been essential to a wide variety of cultures for millennia because they provide young people with meaningful rites of passage to assist them in the transition into adulthood through an empowering and transformationally challenging ordeal. This is something that our culture unfortunately fails to provide to us in our youth, unless we can intuitively create such rites of passage on our own, perhaps through principles taught by Outward Bound,[82] and the vision quest journeys that are provided, for example, by the School of Lost Borders[83] in the wilderness of southeast California. Ed and I subconsciously co-created such an initiation ritual in our spiritual pilgrimage from Massachusetts to Alabama, discussed in *Food for Freedom*, for which I'm deeply grateful, and some of us do find ways to leave our culture and head into the beckoning unknown. Opening to challenges and to discovery, we can return to our culture enriched with inner understandings that we can share with others. Another example is the story of a young man in France, related in the book *Deer Man*, who leaves society to live in the forest with roedeer.[84] Meaningful rites of passage in nature can contribute significantly to our overall health and to the health of our culture. Most of us seem to be at least subliminally aware of this loss of meaningful rituals of passage in our lives. Hopefully we will begin to value the power of introspection in the womb of nature, and how that can support the authentic health of our being, which requires that we strive to fulfill an inspiring purpose throughout our life.

This is actually one of the most important keys to radiant health: living every day as a precious opportunity to learn, grow, and fulfill our unique purpose. We are all going to leave this body, and the inescapable reality of transiency can bring poignancy and grace into our lives. We value flowers and savor their presence because of their transiency, which can never be duplicated by plastic versions. Our days are actually quite few on this Earth, even if we live many years in human terms. When the oldest living person on Earth was asked about her life, the 117-year-old woman replied, "It seemed rather short."[85] Our life passes quickly and we are not on this Earth merely to transmit our genes and then pass on. We are here to fulfill a calling which we alone can envision, understand, and strive to accomplish. Our body is our vehicle for this and that is its sacred purpose.

When we do the inner work to cultivate a vibrant sense of our life purpose, we naturally, every morning, awaken with a sense of appreciation for another day, and consciously give thanks for the opportunity to discover, evolve, contribute, and fulfill our mission for this lifetime during the coming day. This sets the tone, and reverberates not just through the rest of the day, but also throughout our entire body, invigorating every cell, organ, and system, all of which have, as their prime objective, to aid us in the successful fulfilment of our mission. When we are relishing and valuing our life, and striving to do the best we can to awaken our highest potential for the benefit of all living beings, every aspect of our body-mind is enrolled and will loyally serve the cause to which we are dedicated. Nature's inherent wisdom reminds us of this. The ongoing inspiration coming from our heart's commitment to living authentically is an essential foundation for a healthy body. Our spirituality connects us to our mission, which our body is created to facilitate and serve.

Living With the Earth

All the aspects of wellness that we have been discussing—mindful and compassionate nutrition, meditation and self-inquiry, conscious relationships, healthy movement and exercise, and authentically connecting with nature—are ultimately guided by our purpose in this life. This purpose evolves and is fulfilled every day through the challenges, opportunities, and transitions we are creating and experiencing, though we are being continually bombarded with media, education, and cultural messages that are antithetical to this. We are being relentlessly coerced to abandon our purpose, to see ourselves as mere material objects, to seek comfort, acceptance, safety, and approval, to avoid frightening situations, and to serve agendas that are contrary to our mission. This leads to confusion, loss of self-respect, and, to escape the pain of it, to indulgence in addictive substances, further hampering our health and awareness.

The actions and messages we are transmitting to our cells, organs, and systems confuse them also. All our thoughts and emotions are impressed on the living substance of our physical vehicle, and we see it all manifested in our body and affairs, whether it is disharmony and disease, or the harmony and ease that flow from taking responsibility for every aspect of our lives. While we might not be able to control what is happening in the world around us, we can control our responses to these happenings. We can take responsibility for what we bring to situations, and for the thoughts that we entertain, and on what we focus our attention, and to what we pledge our loyalty. We have capacities far beyond what we realize, and our connection with nature is an essential ally in staying connected to the deeper wisdom that guides us to more fully realize our true nature. Walt Whitman sums it well in these two lines from his poem, "Song of the Open Road:"

Now I see the secret of the making of the best persons,
It is to grow in the open air and to eat and sleep with
the earth.

Nature provides whatever we need for healing. It is through poisoning nature and our body-minds with toxic chemicals, electromagnetic fields, and deluded technological narratives that most of our disease arises. Water, especially cold water, is a potent ally in healing. I discovered this over forty years ago when I began seeking every day to immerse myself in cold natural water, like the Pacific Ocean or the streams running down Mount Tamalpais in Marin County north of San Francisco. Since then, nearly every day, this has been a valuable ritual that has led me to swimming in lakes, rivers, and streams all over the Americas and Europe, as well as in Asia, Africa, and Australia. The universal benediction that living water confers has been remarkably consistent. It dissolves the built-up toxicity of electromagnetic radiation, cleanses the energy field, and dissipates lurking disharmonies, bringing joy, vitality, and renewal to all aspects of body and mind. Cold water rejuvenates even more, stimulating the tens of thousands of miles of blood and lymphatic vessels and invigorating our nervous system and immune system, and bringing clarity to our mind and senses. One of the great difficulties we face is that animal agriculture relentlessly pollutes the streams, rivers, lakes, and oceans of our world, not only harming and killing marine life and ecosystems, but making it more difficult for us to partake of the potent healing gifts these waters offer us.

Nature is always beckoning us to awaken from the cultural trance that defines us, and that prohibits us from fully seeing and understanding the splendor and magnificence of free-living animals and the natural world. I got a glimpse of this back in the early 1980s when I was living in the San Francisco Bay area and my old Zen teacher told me about an ancient meditation practice that he had done as a young man where one walks for 72 hours without stopping. I decided to undertake the practice and began my 72-hour walking meditation in the small back yard of the house in which I was living, a roughly circular path that went around a large plum tree. It was a remarkable and challenging experience. After 12 hours of walking, nightfall was coming on, and I still had 60 hours to go and realized how difficult this would be. The nights were especially demanding and seemed to go on forever, and it was difficult to see and keep my bearings. By late afternoon on the second day, I was severely sleep-deprived and noticed that the flowers blossoming off to my right were unlike any I had ever seen. They positively glowed with a brilliant inner luminescence that was startling to behold. After darkness set in again, the plum tree began to come alive to my perception, not in the usual biological sense of being alive, but alive in the sense of manifesting itself to me as a living and aware being that was dancing silently in the dim light of the night, and that inspired a sense of wonder and respect. The tree had a majestic and conscious, living presence, and this experience seared a new understanding into my heart and mind, that trees are not merely biologically alive, but are actually conscious living beings as well.

From the time I was an infant I had been raised in a cultural milieu that narrowed my field of awareness and confined my vision to the outer material shell of the living world. Now I was getting a glimpse of a deeper and poignant reality, and I'm grateful for the challenge of the 72-hour walking meditation. Even now, four decades later, I have a sense of the abiding presence of the benevolent tree-beings with whom we share this planet. I have resisted the temptation to use hallucinogenic mushrooms and other plants and substances as many people do to escape the confines of culturally-indoctrinated reality, and have preferred to work directly with consciousness through meditation and physical practices, like this walk. Though I have only scratched the surface of the deep wisdom and power of nature, and its capacity to bring well-being into my life, the insights gained have been liberating, and have at least kept me out of pharmacies the past fifty years.

Even if we have difficulties finding our way to natural wilderness, due to various reasons and logistical challenges, we can, wherever we are, discover and bring the healing power of nature into our living spaces. We can have plants in our homes, naturally cleansing and oxygenating the air, and all manner of art, artifacts, decorations, and furnishings that invoke the presence of nature, and are perhaps fashioned from whole and ethically-sourced branches, rocks, shells, and so forth. We can appreciate and communicate with the wildlife right where we live, like the spiders who weave their exquisite webs, and the various birds, bees, and other creatures who are our neighbors, even in urban environments.

Each one of us is a magnificent manifestation of nature, and our bodies are kin to the bodies of all living beings. We are healed by reconnecting authentically with the natural world that supports us every moment of every day. Even though as a culture and as individuals we have lost our way, and exploit and dominate nature, it is not helpful to think of ourselves as a plague, virus, or cancer on the Earth as many do. Though we are wounded by our conditioning, we have opportunities every day to savor the presence of the sky, the sun, the moon, the clouds, the stars, the breeze, the rain, and the flowers, trees, birds, squirrels, streams, and natural beauty that is all around us, and is mirrored in our fingers, eyes, lips, and hearts, and in our irresistible yearning to create, learn, care, explore, and understand more deeply.

Willow Wisdom

There she stands by the slowly river
No longer only reaching high:
Rooted in the warm dark earth
That holds and nurtures everything.
She reaches up like other trees to heaven,
To freedom, light, and joy,
And yet returns her gracious boughs
To touch the earth and stream again.
Weeping tears of empathy,
She bends low to caress the earth,
To enter fully the world again,
With gift-bestowing hands

Chapter Six

THE SIXTH KEY: THE HEALING POWER OF CREATIVITY

"Beauty is truth, truth beauty, —that is all
Ye know on earth, and all ye need to know."
—JOHN KEATS

"Music is a moral law. It gives soul to the universe, wings to the
mind, flight to the imagination, and charm and gaiety to life and
to everything."
—PLATO

Remember the clear light,
The pure clear white light,
From which everything in the universe comes,
To which everything in the universe returns:
The original nature of your own mind.
The natural state of the universe unmanifest.
Let go into the clear light, trust it, merge with it.
It is your own true nature; it is home.
—THE TIBETAN BOOK OF THE DEAD

Creativity: A Path to Healing

The sixth and final key to healthy living is creative expression. We all know we have a unique song within us, and that as we discover our song and present it to the world, we find meaning and authenticity enriching our lives. Failing to discover and sing our song, we find depression, anxiety, and despair. This idea is well expressed in the gnostic Gospel of Thomas: "Jesus said, 'If you bring forth what is within you, what you bring forth will save you. If you do not bring forth what is within you, what you do not bring forth will destroy you.'"[86]

It is our inner wisdom—what I call Sophia in *The World Peace Diet*, our intuition—that whispers to us and guides us every day in our quest to deepen our connection with our purpose, and with the contributions that we are uniquely called to bequeath to our world. So, every day, we can take time to be creative in whatever ways call to us: dance, imagine, collaborate, sing, write, paint, design, knit, compose, amuse, invent, inspire, build, play a musical instrument, prepare food, speak up, organize, dream, improvise, teach, journal, repair, craft, caress, respond, communicate, question, create. This is our work on this Earth. Creativity is the overflowing of life into the greater life, for the sharing, healing, and celebrating of our life together.

Our creativity fosters connectedness. Some of our creative efforts seem quite solitary, like composing a poem, or painting a watercolor, and others are more obviously collaborative, but even in our more solitary endeavors, we are connected with, and both expressing and influencing, our fellows and our culture. All creativity is in many ways co-creativity, and it not only connects us with others and with our purpose, but also with meaning and with the joy that continually bubbles at the core of our being. In creativity we fulfill our purpose, and the more deeply we live the truth that we are, the more powerfully we encourage others to do the same. Our authentic gusto-filled life is one of the greatest ongoing creative gifts we can bestow on those around us.

If we are merely activists who are intent on changing other people, we confine ourselves to the shallows and reduce others to objects to be manipulated, eroding the potential for authentic connectivity with them. Understanding this helps us to deepen our practice of listening to others and connecting with them creatively as people, and sharing our experience without trying to change them. This vital human spark fosters spontaneity and caring, and feeds not just our own hearts, but others as well. Without this understanding of creativity and connectedness, we find that frustration builds, as well as the possibility of burnout, and despite the apparently good intentions underlying our activism, we end up paradoxically increasing the resistance, suffering, and disharmony in the world. Imaginatively putting ourselves in others' shoes nourishes our compassion and creativity, and paradoxically increases our effectiveness in liberating animals and all of us.

We have all experienced being creative in a wide variety of ways, not just through music, art, dance, writing, humor, or design, but through our daily interactions and conversations with people, and making our way in the world. Life is inherently improvisational, and improvisation is an expression of our innate creative potential. Each life is unique, and each of us has our particular talents and tendencies.

For myself, many lessons and insights about the healing power of creativity have revolved around writing, and even more so, through music. Over the years, I've experienced the power of music to inspire and heal, and also to open inner and outer doorways to greater awareness and opportunities. While creating music has been one of the greatest keys to freedom, meaning, and joy in my life, in many ways, it seems I have only glimpsed the surface of the vast potentials it holds. Some of my earliest memories are of my father at the piano. Besides being a writer and journalist, he was also an accomplished pianist who before marriage had started a dance band and loved to play Gershwin and the big band standards of his generation. As a child I liked to be like him and play the piano, and he became my first teacher, continually reminding me of the importance of daily practice as the key to musical development. With time I gradually improved to the point where I was giving piano recitals, and in high school was a church organist. In college, I played for musicals and undertook more training, and began yearning to create music, and this led to improvising at the piano and to composing. At the same time, and spurred by the music I was playing and exploring, I developed a thirst for spiritual teachings and practices, and learned to enter a somewhat meditative state while playing the piano. By deliberately pausing the thinking process, I learned to allow melodic, rhythmic, and harmonic patterns to emerge and flow through me.

This experience was remarkably inspiring, and at times I felt I was connecting with benign forces that were helping me understand myself and the world more deeply, and also healing old wounds from childhood. It was part of a larger quest, which involved reading eagerly in world religious literature, beginning to meditate regularly, and questioning official narratives. All of this eventually led to the spiritual pilgrimage my brother Ed and I took, leaving our family home in Concord, MA, and walking south to The Farm in Tennessee, and on to Alabama, and living in meditation centers for about five years, with the music somewhat in the background, but always present. Whenever I could find a piano, I would avidly play and improvise, and this led to an expanding capacity to create original pieces, and eventually, in my late twenties, in northern California, to presenting concerts and producing albums of original piano music.[87]

People were often touched by what they said was an unusually uplifting quality to the music and would purchase the cassette recordings, and this became an increasingly significant source of income. Throughout my doctoral studies in education at U.C., Berkeley, which required an enormous amount of reading and writing, the music continued to beckon and inspire. During and following the years in graduate school, I was blessed with opportunities to teach a wide variety of subjects at several colleges and universities in the San Francisco Bay area, including an assortment of philosophy and humanities courses, as well as courses in creativity, comparative religion, mythology, music, art, film, history, literature, and creative writing. Despite my love for teaching, I eventually felt that it was time to make a leap and leave academia, and to try something new. Converting my 1971 VW bus into a little house on wheels, I traveled North America for about three years presenting concerts of original piano music as well as workshops on developing intuition, which had been the focus of my Ph.D. dissertation. Though it took a lot of effort to arrange the events, overall, it seemed to be a remarkable success. The recordings and donations covered living expenses, and I saw how the thousands of hours of practicing the piano, and later of practicing meditation, were now allowing new vistas of freedom to unfold, not just from academic bureaucracy, but also to be able to create more authentically, and to have more free time for connecting with nature and for meditation, reading, and study. I was grateful for the blisscipline that conferred such happiness and opportunity.

Creativity, Intuition, and Spirituality

I have found that creativity, intuition, and spirituality are all deeply connected, and I refer to them as the Three Sisters. All three tend to lead into healing. When we are living in alignment with our intuition and with our purpose, it seems that synchronicities begin to blossom, and, as Joseph Campbell put it, "doors open where there were no doors." Living in the VW bus, I decided to set up a lecture and concert tour through Unity churches in the eastern U.S., and in the autumn of 1990 embarked on a two-year tour, with the second stop a Unity center in the Toronto area. The same weekend at the center, another guest presenter—a noted intuitive teacher named Paul Solomon, who had founded The Fellowship of the

Inner Light in Virginia Beach—presented a workshop on abundance. About forty people were in attendance. We had had no conversations about anything, though at one point I provided some musical accompaniment to a meditation he led.

Toward the end of his workshop in the afternoon, I remember sitting in the back of the room when he suddenly, seemingly from nowhere, announced to everyone, "There is a man here who is an intuitive musician, a pianist of the soul, and he can tune into your essence and create your soul's music, and you will find it beneficial and healing. His name is Will Tuttle." He then just continued on with his prior train of thought, and though I was somewhat amazed at what he had just said, I smiled inside, because I knew that it was true. He had just planted a seed and it is still bearing fruit over thirty years later. After the workshop was over, several people approached me requesting a personalized music session and recording. I quickly went to a music store to purchase the needed microphones and recording equipment, and from that weekend on, every Sunday at a Unity church in a different city on the tour I had arranged, I would take appointments for individual sessions of personalized piano music and create original recordings for interested people. It turned out that people regularly signed up for them, and the positive response was significant.

With the years of meditation training, I was able to enter a receptive state and connect with the person's essence, beyond the level of the personality. Then, invoking the intention of being a conduit for music that would support the highest unfoldment on every level for the person involved, and for all beings, I would start playing the piano, allowing the person's spirit to pull the unique music out of me, following it and playing for typically about thirty minutes. All of the melodies, rhythms, and harmonies would be recorded so the person (or couple) could bring the music home with them on a cassette, and then later, on a CD, and still later, as a download. I directly witnessed music's transformational potential, and heard from people that experiencing their unique music helped with emotional, relationship, career, and physical challenges they were experiencing.

During this time, I went to the Soviet Union to play several concerts as part of a citizen diplomacy effort to reduce hostility and foster friendship between our two nations, and following that, traveling around Europe, I stopped for a few days in central Switzerland. One evening, as I played the piano at an art gallery opening, a local watercolor artist attending came over to me and asked if she could buy a recording of my music. She seemed moved by the music and I eventually found out when she came to the U.S. from Switzerland a couple of years later that from the time she was a young girl, she had heard in her mind a haunting melody and had been searching for it ever since. When I played the piano at the gallery, she felt she had at last found the music for which she had been searching. For me, musical creativity has brought many gifts, but the most precious gift music has bequeathed is my beloved spouse, Madeleine. She recognized the music, and it brought us together. She came to California in 1992 and began contributing her intuitive ability as a watercolor artist, creating album covers, art cards, and paintings. We married and decided to take our musical and artistic creativity on the road, living and traveling in an RV rolling home for 17 years, presenting concerts, workshops, exhibits, and Sunday morning presentations at churches, conferences, and spiritual centers around North America. Most every week we took appointments for creating individualized music and art portraits for individuals and couples. We have now created thousands of these, and still hear from people how they have benefitted from the art and music that came through us for them.[88] We also create them for companion animals such as dogs, cats, and horses, and find a similarly unique individual presence inspiring us.

It became clear that being a conduit for healing music for others was also healing for me as well. Besides being an opportunity to practice the art of looking beyond the outer form of a person to connect with, and musically express, his or her essential being, it called for learning to open and dedicate the body-mind to be an instrument to benefit others. I have found that these practices generate a healing field that facilitates embarking on spontaneous adventures into both musical and metaphysical realms. We become what we practice, and with practice, we can open to musical, artistic, intuitive, and spiritual capacities that allow us to embark on improvisational excursions that bring cascading therapeutic effects. The benefits overflow into the mental, emotional, physical, and energetic dimensions of our being, and bless both the musician artists and those on the receiving end as well. In many ways, what appears to be creativity is more accurately understood as learning to get out of the way, and to be a faithful instrument for a higher power to flow through, and in this, the apparent recipients are also co-creators or (co-conduits) as well. The deeply-entrenched materialism of our culture has regrettably blinded us to the significant beneficial potentials of creativity when it is combined with healing intentionality. Fortunately, this is something we can all explore and cultivate in our own lives in a myriad of ways.

Vibration, Frequency, and Resonance

British biologist Rupert Sheldrake's research has led him to posit that we humans, and all animals, are interconnected through resonant fields that we influence with our thoughts, feelings, and behaviors. We are influenced by these fields as well, which he refers to as morphogenetic fields.[89] Though they are non-physical, and thus non-existent to scientism, their presence helps to explain many phenomena that are currently unexplainable by mainstream science. As Nikola Tesla emphasized, confining our understanding of ourselves and the universe to mere materiality collapses our intelligence and capacities. Tesla especially urged us to explore the deeper underlying patterns that we can sense also through music, and his famous dictum points the way: "If you want to find the secrets of the universe, think in terms of energy, frequency and vibration."

An intriguing key to vitality is making an effort to understand vibration, frequency, rhythm, and resonance. As many branches of wisdom traditions have recognized, with their emphasis on light and sound meditation practices, we are vibratory beings. We can explore this at the physical level, understanding that our body is composed of countless dynamically interplaying patterns of rhythm: hormonal, circadian, circulatory, respiratory, brain-wave, and many more, including the nano-rhythms at the molecular and atomic levels. We are also vibratory beings at the level of consciousness, and our thoughts, emotions, and aspirations have vibratory qualities as well. When we raise our vibratory frequency to higher levels, especially regarding our thoughts and feelings, we naturally find that we begin to resonate with higher frequency phenomena in our environment, and are naturally drawn to beauty, harmony, loving thoughts and actions, healthy foods, and uplifting relationships and living spaces. However, virtually all of us are being bombarded with messages—from government, media, music, billboards, and our culture in general[90]—that are filled with low-vibratory frequencies such as fear, sexual lust, competition, hatred, pride, envy, aggression, attraction to addictive substances, and other messaging designed to divide and numb us, to sell products of dubious value, and to keep us easily managed, addicted, and controlled.

If we allow our vibratory frequency to fall, we tend to resonate with these harmful delusions and temptations, and find our health being eroded, because dis-ease is basically a vibratory state that is disharmonious and operates at a low level, in which we are neglecting to take responsibility for the quality of our consciousness and our relationships. We begin to see ourselves as powerless victims, which is exactly the aim of the underlying agenda of the advertising campaigns and messaging being directed at us, not just through the medical, media, and governmental institutions, but through education and even in some religions as well. Ultimately, our health is our responsibility, as is our vibratory level, both of which are intimately interconnected. Without responsibility, there is no freedom. The more we rise in awareness and respond fully and responsibly to the ongoing stream of challenges and opportunities, the more freedom lives in us, and flows through us into the web of relations that affects everyone.

Through creativity, as well as through the other keys we have been discussing, we naturally raise our vibratory level. We learn to explore our self-nature as consciousness, and through our imagination, we discover new possibilities, insights, and contributions to uplift and heal ourselves and others. When Madeleine tunes in to a person and begins painting, her intuitive and artistic capacities combine to paint a work of art with a variety of symbolic images that manifest in an array of unique motifs, and all the different hues and colors have their particular vibratory tone and timbre, as do the images. When we behold creative works, such as paintings, poems, symphonies, concerts, dances, architectural structures, and so forth, we are opening our consciousness to the vibratory realities that are being expressed and experienced.

Creativity is a big responsibility. When I am creating music, either for an individual, or in a concert setting, I understand how important it is that my intention be set at the highest level possible at the beginning and throughout the entire creation, and that the various aspects of the musical and energetic expression be for the highest good of all. When we create, we have unique possibilities to influence others throughout the web of relations, and this is an elevated calling. We can see, however, that we are often surrounded by creations that do the opposite of uplifting and healing. Commercial music and songs are often filled with harsh and disempowering rhythms, words, and disharmonies, and modern art, architecture, fashion, and even dance seem to similarly grate against our sensibilities and promote mechanical, clashing, and jarring motifs that drain our energy, destabilize and confuse us, and reduce our awareness and vitality.

We have long recognized the power of the arts, from rulers in ancient China who sent ministers out into the villages to listen to the peoples' music to ascertain their level of happiness, to Pythagoras and Plato who emphasized how the arts and music deeply affect and condition us individually and collectively. Joseph Farrell writes, "Art, and music, are potent forms of mind manipulation and social engineering... With enough exposure to ugliness, the soul becomes ugly."[91] As an example, he discusses a letter allegedly written by a music industry executive insider who in 1991 attended a meeting where it was decided that gangster rap music would be strongly promoted because the music industry was heavily invested in the private prison industry. Music industry executives surmised that by promoting music celebrating violence, they could rapidly increase the prison population and thus their income, and also target minorities and lower economic classes, thus further dividing society and increasing profitability. As we know, gangster rap music proliferated, the private prisons filled as incarceration rates climbed, and stereotypes were deepened and reinforced.[92]

Similarly, architecture, aptly called "frozen music," is often harmful to our health on many levels. We are dwarfed into insignificance by massive structures, and disconnected from nature by artificial boxes, barriers, and walls. Like much of modern music, modern art and film tend to be degrading to our sensibilities, and are often intentionally designed to be so.[93] All of this increases profitability for the tiny minority controlling narratives and financial, governmental, medical, media, and academic institutions, as well as the power in their hands to manage perception and maintain control.

We are called to be creative and co-creative, and to envision and create beauty in movement, music, art, architecture, food, design, and in everything we do. When we are beholding and experiencing the cultural artifacts around us, it behooves us to be mindful, and to protect ourselves from the harmful effects that low-vibrational, ugly, and damaging art, music, film, architecture, and other cultural creations would impose on us. Through cultivating meditative awareness, conscious breathing, and the other practices we have been discussing, we keep our vibratory frequency high, and prevent these influences from pulling us down to a lower resonance level. We are called to be proactive, and to protect ourselves and our loved ones, and everyone around us, as much as possible, from low-vibrational, fear- and separation-based creations. One of the best ways to do this is to be creative ourselves, and create not only art, music, dance, writing, clothing, and architecture that uplift, educate, and bring out the best in ourselves and others, but also consciously create our way of being in the world: our gestures, words, and the space we create around us wherever we are and wherever we go. We are always creating because thoughts and actions are creative. Freeing ourselves from cultural indoctrination and habitual thinking, we can raise our awareness and our health, and contribute to a healthier world for everyone.

An example that elucidates how the vibratory resonance of our consciousness may influence our experience of reality comes from the Tibetan Buddhist tradition, which teaches that when our consciousness leaves the body at death, we go to an intermediate state between incarnations. If we fail to recognize the inevitable appearance of the clear light as our true nature, we will be shown, in succession, a series of six lights of different colors—dull white, green, yellow, blue, red, and smoky gray—and we will find ourselves resonantly attracted to one of them, and this resonant attraction will cause us to be born in the realm to which that colored light corresponds. These six possible realms for rebirth are those of the three upper realms—devas (gods), asuras (demigods), and humans—and those of the three lower realms: animals, pretas (hungry ghosts), and denizens of hell. At the time of the great change called death, the vibratory field of our accumulated experience and awareness resonates in such a way that we will yearn to experience the peace and harmony of devas, or the competitive power-battles of the asuras, or the varied possibilities of the human realm, or the many difficulties of the animals, or the relentless craving of the hungry ghosts, or the pain and suffering of one of the hell realms.

All of these realms are temporary, and again, according to our vibratory resonance, we will eventually die in that realm, enter the intermediate state again, be drawn again to a certain vibratory realm and be born there and experience it. According to these teachings, this continues for eons until we awaken out of the delusion of being an essentially separate object self, and as with other spiritual traditions, the emphasis is on cultivating compassion and raising our vibratory frequency beyond self-centered desires and aversions. Like spiritual teachings from many traditions, the six realms can be seen metaphorically as well, representing our daily life experiences. For example, with craving and fear, we find ourselves in the hungry ghost realm; with anger, in a hell realm; with comfortable ease, the deva realm; with competitive aggression, the asura realm, and so forth. It is a universal teaching that our outer experiences tend to reflect our emotional and mental vibratory frequency, and if we are attentive, we can see how inner changes are mirrored by corresponding changes in our outer world.

The point is that we are in many ways projecting our inner reality onto our perceptual field, and into the body of our affairs, according to the vibratory resonance of our awareness, which is a result of our thoughts, feelings, attitudes, actions, and the accumulated seeds we have sown in all these ways. We are creative, often far more than we realize, and we also create the state of health or disease we are experiencing. From a larger perspective, we are not victims of circumstance. Perhaps, at what we could call the soul level, we have chosen a particular disease, disability, or accident in order to learn and grow from the challenge, and to awaken other aspects of our capacities that would otherwise remain latent. Or perhaps we subconsciously yearn for an illness or condition to expe-rience another reality and are resonantly attracted to it, as we are drawn to a particular light in the intermediate state. Even though it brings suffering, we resonate with it. There may be a learning. We may long for a dramatic change in our life and manifest an accident. We may yearn for attention, or to be relieved of certain respon-sibilities, or to receive more sympathy and caring, or to punish ourselves or others, and manifest a chronic condi-tion that fulfills this desire. There are payoffs in all kinds of situations and events, even in apparently negative ones. It is essential that we clarify our consciousness and realize the creative power that is our essential nature. Creativity is the essence of our being, and though our creative bril-liance is in many ways suppressed in our culture and upbringing, it simmers and shines just below the surface of our awareness. We are always creating our experience, moment by moment, and our challenge is to use our gifts for the highest good of all.

Truth is Beauty, and Beauty Truth

Keats reminds us that beauty is truth, and truth beau-ty.[94] When we do our best to create beauty in art, dance, music, writing, food, relationships, and in everything we do, we are reflecting the truth of our being, and savor-ing and serving the highest virtues of kindness, respect, and harmony. We can see these reflected in the natural world around us when our eyes open to the deeper reali-ties by which we are continually sustained. Beauty leads unfailingly to truth, and what is true resonates with the wisdom of our original nature. Traveling the world, for example, what strikes me most about animal agriculture is its relentless ugliness. Animals confined in cages and fences, the pervasive fear and frustration, the inevitable knives and gushing blood, the globs of flesh on dirty cement floors, the stink and nausea of unnatural confinement and toxic chemicals, the harsh sounds of machines, and of desperate mothers and terrified offspring, living beings reduced to lifeless objects, and all sustained by deception. The corollary to Keats: ugliness is deception, and deception ugliness. As we awaken out of deception and out of contributing to ugliness, and quiet our minds and raise our vibratory resonance, we are naturally drawn to beauty and to truth, and to the healing that these offer on every level.

Music can be a remarkable well of revelation, illumining the hidden patterns, principles, and understandings that bring differences together in harmonious and dynamic unity, inspiring communities, songs, and dances that bring beauty to our Earth. Our purpose and humanity's purpose synchronize and unfold ever more fully when we make the effort to transcend self-oriented misunderstandings, and to reclaim the original brightness of our minds and hearts, working to build a world that cares for everyone. We each have our unique song to sing in this effort, and as each of us discovers our song and presents it faithfully, fulfilling our inner calling, we reveal doorways that benefit others.

Our aesthetic sense will unfailingly bring us home to truth, and to the healing awareness of our right relationship with the created order. Growing and preparing plant-sourced foods that are offered by nature can easily be a celebration of beauty and abundance. We are beauty, and yet, when we see clearly, we realize also how essentially ugly our technologies typically are, both in their outer appearance and in their effects on our sensibilities. Science first emerged as a product of the early herding cultures, to facilitate manipulating and breeding animals, and dominating nature. A new way, which is an ancient way, is calling. Spirituality, simplicity, beauty, harmony, and truth build upon each other, and bring creativity and healing into our lives.

We close with this passage from our book on developing intuition, *Your Inner Islands:*

> We leave you with this image for your muse to contemplate: a beautiful grand piano on a stage in a great hall filled with hundreds of eagerly expectant ears, and the musician, seated, launches into the music, but only plays one note. Over and over again, the same note, a B-flat, one note out of the eighty-eight on the keyboard. Alone, isolated, what little power this one note has, what little energy to evoke feeling, meaning, and inspiration! The audience's attention drifts and becomes perturbed as the musician plays only the same poor B-flat note over and over. People are looking at the exit doors when to their great relief another musician appears and displaces the first at the keyboard.
>
> This musician begins with the same ineffectual B-flat note, but moves on, up and down the keyboard, fingers flying as an enormous tide of music pours out of him through the piano and fills the room. The B-flat is now but one among many notes, and yet what power she has,

what force! In certain passages, when her unique voice is heard among the others, there is such poignancy, then again, later, such pathos, and then again, such soaring joy! Her energy and power are now fully displayed, and they come from two things: she is true to herself and, too, she is part of something greater than herself and is true to that as well. Alone, she has little power, but together with the other notes, her potential is limitless. As she sounds her B-flat voice truly and faithfully, and as the other notes do as well, the whole keyboard responds to the musician's touch, and every note contributes to the power and richness of every other note. Together they can build a creation of beauty and feeling that is boundless in its potential.

So, discover your own note, your unique voice, and contribute it, and you will know the source of all energy, the heart of the music, and the relationship of the notes. May your dance create a field of freedom that will bless everyone.[95]

CONCLUSION

"The state of consciousness that we maintain is shown forth in the body that we present to the world."
—Joel Goldsmith

The unique song and resonance that vibrates at the center of our being is ever guiding us to higher perspectives and to a deeper understanding of the vast creative powers that dwell within us. The most valuable gift we offer others is our own life example, lived authentically, and doing our best to fulfill our psychological and spiritual potential for the benefit of all.

As individual expressions of eternal consciousness, we are born into the psychologically and spiritually challenging setting of a late-stage materialistic empire saturated with ten thousand years of relentless and routine violence toward animals for food and other uses. Understanding that humanity's unapologetic abuse of billions of animals daily has brought us to the immense challenges we face today, and how they are a direct result of the mentality required by animal agriculture, we can bring healing to ourselves and to our world on many levels.

While *Food for Freedom* and *The World Peace Diet* have discussed all this and the causes and effects of our current situation in detail, *The World Peace Way* has attempted to simply illuminate the many practical tools at our disposal to deepen, embody, and celebrate this understanding. Doing so, we can savor our beautiful opportunity on this Earth, and respond to the challenges here with vitality, clarity, and compassion.

Our health and freedom are completely intertwined not only with each other as members of the human family, but also with the animals of this Earth as members of the family of living sentient beings. Ultimately, responsibility for the health of our body, mind, and relationships is with us, and by making an effort, moment by moment, hour by hour, and day by day, we can gradually and inexorably raise our consciousness, bringing it ever more into alignment with the Source of our life. The practical suggestions in this book can be remarkably helpful when they are activated and guided by the inner yearning that lives in our heart.

It is this yearning that gives rise to one of the essential virtues: diligence. If we lack diligence, we are easily distracted, deceived, weakened, and defeated by inner and outer obstacles. However, with sufficient diligence, we can transform weakness into strength, fear into courage, and overcome virtually all obstacles that come our way. Diligence ensures progress and brings the highest rewards in every area of life, especially with regard to spiritual development and awakening. It arises from the yearning we feel in the depth of our being to unfold our capacities for the benefit of all living beings.

For this reason, we are naturally motivated to engage in the inner work of clarifying our ideals and our mission, and to continually build the living foundation for our life, which is the unique vision that inspires us. When this vision is alive in our thoughts and feelings, in our mind and heart, it is also alive in every cell of our being. We are enthusiastic about our life and vision, and this gives rise to what appears to be diligence. We put forth effort because we love to do so, and it is our delight and our truth. Kahlil Gibran summed it thus: "Work is love made visible." This is true not just for outer work but for inner work as well, and through our inner and outer work, we discover what could be called the secret work. This is the grace that flows into our life from the higher dimensions, uplifting and carrying us, opening doors of understanding and opportunity, coming from beyond the personal level. Through committed efforts, we tap into grace, and not only raise our level of health and peaceful joy, but also become empowered transmitters. Our positivity becomes contagious. Without trying, we benefit others and attract helpful support and guidance.

Our yearning is the fuel of consciousness, and it tends to bring results in both the inner and outer worlds. The results of course depend on how we direct it, whether we crave worldly goals and recognition, or desire greater wisdom and compassion. We discover that self-oriented ambitions eventually result in more unsatisfactoriness, and that our outer world is ultimately a mirror of our state of consciousness. The suffering we experience is actually a precious ally because it alone seems to be able to redirect our yearning toward higher objectives, as the

Bible reminds us: "He that soweth to his flesh shall of the flesh reap corruption, but he that soweth to the Spirit shall of the Spirit reap eternal life."

Just as everything we think, say, and do today creates the foundation for the reality that we experience when we wake up tomorrow, our actions and consciousness in this life lay the foundation for our future experiences when we leave this life. Our experience of life reflects our consciousness, and our path is up to us. It is the intensity and direction of our yearning that enables the remarkable progress that is always potentially available, whatever the outer circumstances.

Our philosophy is inevitably reflected in how we wash dishes, relate to each other, and savor and protect the beauty that is all around us. Our life is our practice. Deep thanks, dear reader, for taking this journey to help rescue our world, reclaim our health, and fulfill our destiny as co-creators of a positive future for the children of all living beings. May we continue to do our best to contribute to the awakening of human consciousness on this abundant Earth so that we live as we are intended, in creative harmony with the interconnected web of life that includes and supports us all.

ACKNOWLEDGMENTS

We stand on the shoulders of spiritual luminaries who have graced our Earth in countless forms over centuries and millennia, and have inspired written, oral, and symbolic guideposts to help support us on our way during these culturally chaotic times. The great and often-unrecognized feast of wisdom teachings that is our human heritage draws from East and West, North and South, past and future. Each of us can partake of this feast to the degree that we actually discover, eat, and digest the food, and do not content ourselves with non-nutritious pursuits, or with merely analyzing menus and discussing ingredients.

My heartfelt appreciation to the many noble ones who have blessed this lifetime through their words, example, and vital presence, and inspired the practices, tools, and ideas that have found their way into the pages of this book. It seems presumptuous to begin to single out sages, guides, and highly-evolved beings because they comprise a vast tapestry of interconnected wisdom that defies efforts to be reduced to individual strands, knots, and stitches. The World Peace Way, like a deep river, flows ever on, carrying us, often without our full understanding, to destinies that we are still evolving to comprehend.

In the creation of this book as a doorway onto The World Peace Way, special gratitude goes to Christine and John McClarnon for their unflagging encouragement and editing input, to Britt Lind, Anil Narang, Philip Nicozisis, and Casey Taft for their support and suggestions, and especially to Madeleine, spouse and spiritual companion, for her loving presence and inspiration, and for her art that flows in a wide variety of beautiful expressions.

May all living beings find our way home.

MADELEINE'S INTUITIVE KITCHEN
Happy Dining for Body, Earth, and Spirit

BY MADELEINE TUTTLE

Here are some basic recipes, which can be repeated or mixed and matched in different ways, with a shopping list at the end. We kept the dishes pretty simple, but there is a lot of variety. Please use only whole organic ingredients if possible!

Some meals call for tahini sauce, which is easy to make; just add some water to tahini & stir until smooth. Some call for hemp hearts sauce, blending hemp hearts and water in a blender.

It can be convenient to cook pasta, potatoes, rice, and other grains in a large quantity and store them in the fridge to use later in stir fries, salads, and other meals. Some recipes call for leftover grains.

We purposefully don't mention measurements, just the different ingredients. So let your intuition create wildly and have fun!

I love to "paint" the meals: add paprika if it lacks red, or herbs, baby leaves, or sprouts if it lacks green. Turmeric, curry, or peppers for yellow, and so forth.

- **Favorite breakfast**—a Green Smoothie! Feel great 'til lunch! Blend fruits in season, bananas, citrus, kale or spinach, ginger, flaxseeds (can be ground first in coffee grinder), cinnamon, clove, nuts, & water.
- **Other favorite breakfast**—Non-sweet Cleansing Smoothie! Overnight, soak flaxseeds, chia seeds, black cumin seeds, and several almonds. In the morning, add hemp hearts, ginger, apple, cucumber, celery, whole lemon with rind, and add fresh herbs to taste.
- **Favorite lunch**—Oatley! Soak oat flakes overnight if possible, or at least a couple of hours, add vegan yogurt with fresh fruits in season. Many creative possibilities—see Madeleine's Intuitive Kitchen YouTube channel for enticing options.
- **Other favorite lunch**—Tortillas! Spread tahini sauce or hemp hearts sauce (see above) on a tortilla and fill with lettuce, sprouts, tomatoes, cucumber, walnuts, olives, herbs, spices. Variations: add avocado, tofu, seitan, tempeh, etc.
- **Favorite dinners**—Mashed potatoes topped with veggie ragout. Boil cut-up potatoes in water. When soft, pour most of the water into a bowl and save. Add plant milk, nutmeg, a little tamari, and mash with potato masher. Add some of the water back if necessary. Steam seasonal veggies, and when *al dente* add tahini sauce, tamari, herbs, minced garlic, and mix. Add some herbs and spices to the leftover potato water for a delicious soup. Save leftover mashed potatoes for Shepherd's Pie (below)! Sweet potatoes can be used instead.
- **Spaghetti**—Cook spaghetti with chunks of winter squash in water, and when nearly soft, put broccoli flowers on top. Cover and cook until *al dente*. Pour water off (as a soup) and serve with tomato sauce, or with a grated ginger-tahini sauce (see above).

- **Salad**—Chop and mix greens, peppers, tomatoes, cucumbers, celery, onions, etc.; add tahini sauce, lemon, tamari, herbs, and spices, and mix. Variations: add tofu or tempeh cubes, leftover rice, noodles, kasha, bulgur, or cut-up boiled potatoes, or eat with bread, toast, or crackers.
- **Couscous**—Boil water and pour over couscous in a bowl with added cumin seeds. Sauté onions, squash, cabbage, and a few potato chunks and curry. When soft, add tahini sauce, tamari, ground pepper, mint, and mix. Place in the middle of bed of couscous.
- **Bulgur**—Boil finely cut veggies, turmeric, cumin in water, then add bulgur. Cook about five minutes till soft, and turn off heat. Mix raw spinach leaves under.
- **Polenta**—Boil water with rosemary; with whisker, stir in cornmeal. Steam seasonal veggies, add tofu, and when soft, add tahini sauce, tamari, Italian herb mix, and cayenne. Mix and top over cornmeal.
- **Quinoa**—Boil quinoa in water (approximately 3:1) for 45 minutes. Add kale when 2/3 done. Sauté slices of tempeh, then sauté mushrooms with onions. Top quinoa with sauté and fresh basil.
- **Carrot salad**—Finely grate carrots. Mix tahini sauce with lemon and tamari, add peppermint herb, and pour over grated carrots. Add pine nuts or walnuts.
- **Shepherd's Pie**—Sauté onions and zucchini in a wide shallow pan with lid. Spread peas and crumbled tofu or tempeh, top it with leftover mashed potatoes and cook until warm.
- **Rice**—Cook Lotus brand rice. Mix raw sauce containing finely-cut peppers, celery, tomatoes, parsley, walnuts, olives, lemon, herbs, and spices. Pour over cooked rice, sprinkle with lemon juice.

- **Millet with roasted leek**—Cook millet (4:1) for 30 minutes. Sauté leeks. When soft, add minced garlic and tamari. Serve over millet with a few drops of lemon and toasted sesame oil. Adorn with baby spinach.

- **Pumpkin soup**—Boil Kabocha squash (or other winter squash) in water. When soft, pour into blender. Add a spoonful of tahini and blend until smooth, the briefly blend in fresh cilantro. When served, add a little tamari.

- **Bean tortillas**—Spread fresh cooked or refried beans on tortillas. Cut up cilantro and/or other greens, tomatoes, cucumbers. Add salsa or hemp cream, cayenne, pepper, and roll up.

- **Angel-hair noodles on kale bed**—Cook angel-hair noodles. Steam kale, add roasted sesame seeds, tamari, toasted sesame oil. Serve angel hair on bed of kale, and sprinkle with paprika, toasted sesame oil, tamari, and finally, toasted sesame seeds.

- **Sablé cookies**—Mix spelt flour, Sucanat, vanilla, and a pinch of salt with liquefied coconut oil and water. Shape into long bars 1 1/2 inches in diameter. Put into refrigerator for half hour. When firm, cut into 1/3-inch cookie slices. Put onto baking pan and bake at 350 until light brown (ca. 20-30 minutes). Variation: add hazelnuts or shredded almonds or raisins.

- **Chocolate cookies**—Mix spelt flour, chocolate powder, shredded coconut, crushed walnuts, and a pinch of salt. Add maple syrup or Sucanat and coconut oil. Spread onto baking sheet and bake about 20-30 minutes. When still warm, cut into squares or bars.

* * *

SHOPPING LIST:

Allow yourself a good hour to explore and buy the following items, always *organic*, fair trade, and non-GMO. The more love you feel, the better the outcome.

The best place to "shop" is in your own organic (and veganic) garden. The second-best is at the local farmers' market or through a local CSA or food-co-op. The third best is in the organic section of your local grocery store, or through carefully-vetted online suppliers (see Nutrition and Healthy Living Resources section for suggestions also).

Grains: Lotus brand rice, millet, spaghetti, angel-hair, couscous, quinoa, buckwheat, bulgur, wild rice, cornmeal, oats, beans. (Note: we recommend acquiring a small kitchen grain mill to make fresh flour and cornmeal. Also, a hand-powered flaker to roll/flake the oat grains.)

Veggies: In season, pumpkin/squash, leek, onions, garlic, kale, cabbage, ginger, lemons, broccoli, peppers, mushrooms, carrots, lettuce/greens, sprouts, spinach, tomatoes, cucumbers, celery, avocado, cilantro, peas (fresh or frozen), potatoes, sweet potatoes.

Proteins: Tofu, tempeh, seitan, lentils, split peas, beans, and other legumes.

Herbs & spices—fresh if possible, or dried: peppermint, parsley, basil, dill, cilantro, oregano, sage, rosemary, thyme, turmeric, paprika, cayenne, curry, pepper, nutmeg powder, cumin seeds, cardamon, cinnamon, clove, etc.

Fruits: citrus, apples, bananas, grapes, blueberries, and other fruits & berries in season.

Other: flaxseeds, almonds, walnuts, hazelnuts, pine nuts, raisins, sesame seeds, tahini (sesame butter), tomato sauce, tamari or shoyu, refried beans, Real Salt (from Utah) or sea salt, vanilla, coconut oil, chocolate powder, shredded coconut, maple syrup.

Though there are commercial plant-based cheeses, milks, ice creams, burgers, etc., when ready to go deeper into healthy vegan living, it's best to refrain from processed and non-organic foods.

When you sit down to eat, look at what you created. Enjoy the colors, smells, tastes, and the love that blesses the food. The Oneness of all beings!

Bon Appetit!
Stay in touch—feel free to copy!
For more details and ideas, see Madeleine's Intuitive Kitchen online videos.

RESOURCES

by Dr. Will & Madeleine Tuttle

~⁂~

Available through worldpeacediet.com, willtuttle.com, and relevant online platforms.

AnimalSongs. Music CD by Will Tuttle. Original piano blended with voices of animals; special focus on animals used for food production. 61 mins.

Buddhism and Veganism: Essays Connecting Spiritual Awakening and Animal Liberation. Edited by Dr. Will Tuttle. Essays by internationally recognized Buddhist authors on vegan living and spiritual practice. Vegan Publishers, 2018. 250 pages.

Bursting Light: Favorite Original Piano Solos by Will Tuttle with Visionary Paintings by Madeleine Tuttle. Sheet music for 15 pieces of piano music composed by Will, plus 25 full-color images of paintings by Madeleine. Karuna Music and Arts, 2018. 132 pages.

Circles of Compassion: Essays Connecting Issues of Justice. Edited by Will Tuttle. Essays by internationally recognized authors on the intersectionality of justice issues. Vegan Publishers, 2014. 320 pages.

Conscious Eating: The Power of our Food Choices. DVD by Will Tuttle. Fully illustrated interview, plus three other programs, including a World Peace Diet keynote lecture. 110 mins.

Daily VegInspiration: Jewels from The World Peace Diet. By Dr. Will Tuttle with original art by Madeleine Tuttle. Inspiring excerpts from *The World Peace Diet*, one for every day of the year, embellished with Japanese brush art paintings by Madeleine. Karuna Music and Arts, 2018. 160 pages.

Food for Freedom: Reclaiming Our Health and Rescuing Our World. By Dr. Will Tuttle. Best-selling book focusing on animal liberation as the essential key to human freedom, and uniting the health freedom and vegan movements to heal the divisions in our culture and empower spirituality over materialism. Karuna, 2024. 372 pages.

Four Viharas Guided Meditation. CD by Will Tuttle. Meditation on loving-kindness, compassion, joy, and peace, for cultivating inner and outer harmony, with original piano music. Two versions, one for beginning practitioners, and one for more seasoned. 45 mins.

Living in Harmony with All Life. CD by Will Tuttle. In-depth monologue covering the main ideas presented in *The World Peace Diet*. 75 mins.

Madeleine's Intuitive Kitchen. YouTube channel of videos of healthy organic vegan food preparation by Madeleine Tuttle, including gardening, crafts, exercise, and music. See YouTube listing following.

The World Peace Diet: Eating for Spiritual Health and Social Harmony. By Will Tuttle. International best-selling book translated into 17 languages. This book helped launch the vegan spirituality movement and provides a broad and in-depth overview of the consequences of animal agriculture. Lantern Books, 2005, 2016. 360 pages.

The World Peace Diet audio book. CD by Will Tuttle. Contains the entire *World Peace Diet* text in an unabridged reading by the author. 31 tracks. It is 13.5 hours long, in an MP3 format.

World Peace Diet Circle: Monthly online discussion group—90 minutes typically on the third Thursday of each month: worldpeacemastery.com.

World Peace Diet Mastery and Facilitator Training Programs. Self-paced online training by Will Tuttle. Four-module and eight-module online training by Dr. Will Tuttle, includes audio and video teachings as well as additional resources and monthly online discussion group: worldpeacemastery.com.

World Peace Meditations—Eightfold Path for Awakening Hearts. CD by Will Tuttle. Eight guided meditations with original piano by Will and flute music by Madeleine, plus *World Peace Diet* passages for meditation. 79 mins.

Worldwide Vegan Summit for Truth and Freedom. Directed and produced by Will Tuttle. Eighteen video presentations on health freedom by noted vegan doctors, authors, advocates, and organizers with audio and written transcripts. worldpeacediet.com/worldwide-vegan-summit

Worldwide Prayer Circle for Animals: every day at noon we join together in an affirmative prayer: "Compassion Encircles the Earth for all beings everywhere." See circleofcompassion.org for more information.

Your Inner Islands: The Keys to Intuitive Living by Dr. Will Tuttle. A narrative adventure with teachings and practices to help readers activate the inner guidance system of spiritual intuition. Karuna Music and Arts, 2017. 150 pages.

YouTube video channel with Dr. Tuttle's lectures, presentations, interviews, and concerts, as well as "Madeleine's Intuitive Kitchen" with food, gardening, yoga, and crafts videos by Madeleine Tuttle. See youtube.com/channel/willtuttle

See willtuttle.com and/or worldpeacediet.com for more information on upcoming events, plus essays, writings, meditations, music CDs, art prints, fiber art, individualized music and art portraits, ordering, contacting, and downloading. Books and audio recordings are also available through online commercial sources.

NUTRITION AND HEALTHY LIVING RESOURCES

~

Bibliography

Barnard, Neal. *Power Foods for the Brain: An Effective 3-Step Plan to Protect Your Mind and Strengthen Your Memory*. New York: Grand Central, 2013.

_____. *Your Body in Balance: The New Science of Food, Hormones, and Health*. New York: Grand Central, 2020.

Bragg, Paul and Patricia. *The Miracle of Fasting: Proven Throughout History*. Bragg Fifty-Second edition, 2021.

Brulé, Dan, *Just Breathe: Mastering Breathwork*. New York: Simon & Schuster, 2017.

Burnett, Graham. *The Vegan Book of Permaculture*. Hampshire: Permanent Publications, 2014.

Campbell, T. Colin and Campbell, Thomas. *The China Study: Revised and Expanded Edition: The Most Comprehensive Study of Nutrition Ever Conducted and the Startling Implications for Diet, Weight Loss, and Long-Term Health*. Dallas: BenBella, 2016.

Campbell, T. Colin. *Whole: Rethinking the Science of Nutrition*. Dallas: BenBella, 2013.

Cheeke, Robert and Espinoza, Vanessa. *Plant-based Muscle: Our Roadmap to Peak Performance on a Plant-Based Diet.* Los Angeles: Gaven Press, 2017

Christy, Martha M. *Your Own Perfect Medicine.* Mesa, AZ: Wishland, 1994.

Clement, Brian and Clement, Anne Marie. *Killer Clothes: How Seemingly Innocent Clothing Choices Endanger Your Health...and How to Protect Yourself.* Summertown, TN: Book Publishing, 2011.

_____, *Self-Healing Diet: A Scientifically Supported, Life-Awakening Guide Revealing the Impact Our Lifestyle Choices Have on Our Health, Longevity, and Environment.* Independently Published, 2023.

Cousens, Gabriel. *Conscious Eating.* New York: North Atlantic Books, 2000.

Davis, Brenda, and Melina, Vesanto. *Becoming Vegan: Comprehensive Edition.* Summertown, TN: Book Publishing Company., 2014.

Delorme, Geoffroy. *Deer Man: Seven Years of Living in the Wild.* Greystone Books, 2022 (English translation).

Eddy, Mary Baker. *Science and Health with Key to the Scriptures.* Boston: Christian Science Publishing, 1904, 1934

Ferguson, Anna. *World Peace Yoga.* Cincinnati: Heart Books, 2018.

Fillmore, Charles. *The Twelve Powers.* Unity Spiritual Center: 2015.

Fronsdale, Gil, tr. *The Dhammapada.* Boulder: Shambhala, 2006.

Fuhrman, Joel. *Fast Food Genocide: How Processed Food Is Killing Us and What We Can Do About It* New York: HarperCollins, 2017.

_____. *Fasting and Eating for Health: A Medical Doctor's Program for Conquering Disease*. New York: St. Martin's Press, 1995.

Gannon, Sharon, and Life, David. *Jivamukti Yoga: Practices for Liberating Body and Soul*. New York: Random House, 2002.

Goldsmith, *The Infinite Way*, New York: DeVorss, 1947.

Greger, Michael. *How Not to Die: Discover the Foods Scientifically Proven to Prevent and Reverse Disease*. New York: Flatiron Books, 2015.

Hall, Jenny and Tolhurst, Iain. *Growing Green: Animal-Free Organic Techniques*. White River Junction: Chelsea Green, 2006.

Hanh, Thich Nhat. *Peace is Every Step: The Path of Mindfulness in Everyday Life*. New York: Bantam, 1991.

Heruka, Tsangnyon, tr. *The Hundred Thousand Songs of Milarepa*. Boulder: Shambhala, 2016.

Kahn, Joel. *The Plant-Based Solution: America's Heart Healthy Doc's Plan to Power Your Health*. Boulder: Sounds True, 2018.

Logan, Karen. *Clean House, Clean Planet: Clean Your House for Pennies a Day, the Safe Nontoxic Way*. New York: Simon & Schuster, 1997.

Lisle, Douglas and Goldhamer, Alan. *The Pleasure Trap: Mastering the Hidden Force That Undermines Health & Happiness*. Summertown, TN: Book Publishing, 2003.

Moran, Victoria. *Main Street Vegan*. New York: Tarcher, 2012.

McDougall, John. *The Healthiest Diet on the Planet*. New York: HarperOne, 2016.

_____. *The Starch Solution*. New York: Rodale Press, 2012.

Megré, Vladimir. *Anastasia*. Kahului: Ringing Cedars press, 1996, 2004. This is Book One in this nine-book series, and a tenth book is available as an e-book.

Myers, Toshia and Goldhamer, Alan. *Can Fasting Save Your Life?* Summertown, TN: Book Publishing, 2024)

Nehls, Michael. *The Indoctrinated Brain.* New York: Skyhorse, 2023.

Ober, Clinton, Sinatra, Stephen, and Zucker, Martin. *Earthing: The Most Important Health Discovery Ever?* Laguna Beach: Basic health Publication, 2010.

Ota, Lisa. *The Sacred Art of Eating: Healing Our Relationship with Food.* Sacred Exploration, 2017.

Ozanich, Steve. *Dr. John Sarno's Top 10 Healing Discoveries.* Warren, OH: Silver Cord, 2016.

Pitcairn, Richard and Susan. *Dr. Pitcairn's Complete Guide to Natural health for Dogs and Cats.* New York: Rodale, 2017.

Radzienda, Thomas. *Vegan Health and Spirituality.* Chiang Mai: Sovereign Word Publishing, 2024.

Robbins, John. *The Food Revolution: How Your Diet Can Help Save Your Life and Our World.* New York: Conari, 2010.

Sharma, N.K. *Milk: A Silent Killer.* New Delhi: Life Positive, 2013.

Shelton, Herbert: *Fasting Can Save Your Life.* American Natural Hygiene Society, 1978.

Sherzai, Dean & Ayesha. *The Alzheimer's Solution: A Breakthrough Program to Prevent and Reverse the Symptoms of Cognitive Decline at Every Age.* New York: HarperOne, 2019.

Stevenson, Douglas. *The Farm Then and Now: A Model for Sustainable Living.* Gabriola Island, BC: New Society Publishers, 2014.

Van der kroon, Coen. *The Golden Fountain.* New Delhi: P. Jain Publishers, 1995.

Wigmore, Ann. *The Hippocrates Diet and Health Program.* New York: Avery, 1983.

Online Resources

Environmental Working Group (for checking toxicity of ingredients): ewg.org

Fasting: Dr. Frank Sabatino: drfranksabatino.com

Fasting: Dr. Alan Goldhamer: True North Health Center: healthpromoting.com

Fasting: True North Health Foundation: truenorthhealthfoundation.org

Feel Fabulous with Food: feelfabulouswithfood.com

Food Revolution Network: foodrevolution.org

Healing Power of Flowers with Dr. Rupa Shah: drrupashah.com

Herbal vegan nutrition with Dr. Steve Blake: drsteveblake.com

Hippocrates Wellness: hippocrateswellness.org

Naked Food Magazine: nakedfoodmagazine.com

Organic Consumers Association: organicconsumers.org

Plant-based pharmacist with Dr. Dustin Rudolph: plantbased-pharmacist.com

The Real Truth About Health: therealtruthabouthealth.com

Remineralize the Earth: remineralize.org

School of Lost Borders: schooloflostborders.org

Super Healthy Children: superhealthychildren.com

Switch4Good: switch4good.org

T. Colin Campbell Center for Nutrition Studies: nutrition-studies.org

Vegan Fusion Institute (cooking school): chefmarkreinfeld.com

Vegan nutrition with Evita Ochel: evitaochel.com

Vegan Veterinarian with Dr. Armaiti May: veganvet.net

Foods and Nutrition Sources—U.S.

Azure: organic fresh and packaged food: azurestandard.com

Banyan Botanicals: organic foods, teas, extracts: banyanbotanicals.com

Blue Lotus Chai: organic chai teas: bluelotuschai.com

Chemical-Free Body: organic green powders, de-tox, health: chemicalfreebody.com

Eden Foods: organic grains, beans, seeds, nuts, soy, Japanese products: store.edenfoods.com

Evolution: vegan dog and cat food and treats: petfoodshop. com

Food to Live: organic nuts, seeds, grains, breads, snacks, super-foods: foodtolive.com

Garden of Life: organic meal replacement powder, herbal essences: gardenoflife.com

Go Raw: organic seeds, sprouted bars, granola: goraw.com

HealthForce: organic green powders, cleansing, health: health-forcesuperfoods.com

Hippocrates Wellness: organic raw seeds, foods: store.hippo-crateswellness.org

Lotus Foods: organic rice and noodles: lotusfoods.com

Malama Mushrooms: organic mushroom powder: malama-mushrooms.com

Mocu: organic seeds, mixes, powders, superfoods: mocuhealth. com

Pleasant Hill Grains: organic grains, legumes, seeds: pleasant-hillgrain.com

Real Mushroom: organic mushroom extracts and powders: realmushrooms.com

Simply Organic: organic spices, herbs, extracts: simplyorganic. com

Sprout People: sprouting seeds: sproutpeople.org

Sun Warrior: organic green powders: sunwarrior.com

Terra Soul: organic seeds, nuts, superfoods: terrasoul.com

True Leaf Market: sprouting seeds, microgreens: trueleafmar-ket.com

V-Dog: vegan dog food and treats: v-dog.com

Vitacost: organic packaged foods: Vitacost: vitacost.com

Vitamin Sea Seaweed: wildcrafted sea vegetables: vitaminsea-seaweed.com

Household Sources—U.S.

Azure Clean: all types of organic household and cleaning supplies: azurestandard.com

Chemical-Free Body: sprouting, saunas, water structuring, juicers: chemicalfreebody.com

Clearly Filtered: water purification: clearlyfiltered.com

Coyuchi: organic towels, sheets, blankets, apparel: coyuchi.com

DefenderShield: EMF protection: defendershield.com

E-Cloth: cloth window cleaning kit; sponges: us.e-cloth.com

Epic Water Filters: water purification: epicwaterfilters.com

Fresh and Alive: EMF protection: freshandalive.com

Full Circle Home: kitchen brushes, sponges, compostable food wrap: fullcirclehome.com

Gramicci: organic apparel: gramicci.com

Green Forest Paper: recycled toilet paper, paper towels, facial tissues: greenforestpaper.com

Healthcraft: Surgical steel cookware: healthcraft.com

Hippocrates Wellness: organic bedding, EMF protection, juicing: store.hippocrateswellness.org

If You Care: recycled aluminum foil, compostable parchment paper: buyifyoucare.com

Maggie's Organics: organic socks, apparel, home goods: maggiesorganics.com

Natural Action: water structuring devices: naturalaction.com

Pact: organic towels, sheets, blankets, apparel: wearpact.com

Pleasant Hill Grains: flour mills, flakers, dehydrators, cook's tools: pleasanthillgrain.com

Responsible Products: compostable bags: responsibleproducts.com

Saladmaster: Surgical steel cookware and food processors: saladmaster.com

The Soapy Tree: soap nuts: soapnuts.us

Tribest: juicers, blenders, sprouters, dehydrators, plant-milk makers: tribest.com

Vitamix: blenders, food processors: vitamix.com

Personal Care Sources—U.S.

Desert Essence: shampoo, body care, personal care: desertessence.com

Dr. Bronner: soap, body lotion, lip balm, shampoo, personal care: drbronner.com

Dr. Hauschka: facial, body cleansers, creams; makeup; shampoo, deodorant: drhauschka.com

Eco-Dent: tooth powder, floss: eco-dent.com

Heritage Store: rose water, skin care, shampoos, cosmetics: heritagestore.com

Hippocrates Wellness: skin care, cosmetics: store.hippocrateswellness.org

Nature's Answer: PerioBrite dental cleanse, herbal personal care products: naturesanswer.com

Nature's Brands: organic shampoo, facial creams, cosmetics: naturesbrands.com

OraMD: tooth oil, tooth care: oramd.com

Primal Life Organics: organic dental, toothbrush, cosmetics, skin care: primallifeorganics.com

Weleda: facial and body lotions, oils, and creams; deodorant: weleda.com

Animal Freedom and Sanctuaries

Animal Recovery Mission: animalrecoverymission.org
Animals 24-7: animals24-7.org
Edgar's Mission Animal Sanctuary: edgarsmission.org.au
Farm of the Free Sanctuary: farmofthefree.org
Fish Feel: fishfeel.org
Lei Lanni Farm Sanctuary: leilanifarmsanctuary.org
Peaceful Prairie Sanctuary: peacefulprairie.org
Rowdy Girl Sanctuary: rowdygirlsanctuary.org
United Poultry Concerns: upc-online.org/
Woodstock Farm Animal Sanctuary: woodstockfas.org

NOTES

Preface

1. Steve Ozanich, *Dr. John Sarno's Top 10 Healing Discoveries* (Warren, OH: Silver Cord, 2016)
2. See John Sarno, *The Mindbody Prescription* (New York: Warner, 1998)

Chapter 1—The First Key: Healthy Diet

3. Brian R Clement, *Killer Fish: How Eating Aquatic Life Endangers Your Health*. Hippocrates Publications, 2012.
4. David Wallinga, "U.S. Livestock Antibiotic Use Is Rising, Medical Use Falls," *NRDC,* November 18, 2021. https://www.nrdc.org/bio/david-wallinga-md/us-livestock-antibiotic-use-rising-medical-use-falls-0
5. Joseph Mercola, "Are You Eating Pork Injected with Merck's mRNA Livestock Vaccine?" *Children's Health Defense,* April 10, 2023. https://childrenshealthdefense.org/defender/pork-merck-mrna-livestock-vaccine-cola/
6. Alexandra Caspero and Sarah Klemm, "Building a Healthy Vegetarian Diet: Myths and Facts" *Academy of Nutrition and Dietetics,* October 4, 2021. https://www.eatright.org/food/nutrition/vegetarian-and-special-diets/building-a-healthy-vegetarian-diet-myths
7. Astrid, "6 Little Known Vitamin B12 Rich Foods from Plant Sources," *Heal You Naturally,* January 8, 2021. https://www.healyounaturally.com/vitamin-b12-rich-foods-plant-sources/

8. See Will Tuttle, *The World Peace Diet*, Chapter 5, "The Intelligence of Human Physiology," (New York: Lantern) 2005, 2016, p. 66.

9. Milton Mills, MD, "The Comparative Anatomy of Eating," *Plant-based Nation*, November 15, 2019. https://drmiltonmill-splantbasednation.com/the-comparative-anatomy-of-eating/

10. See T. Colin Campbell, *The China Study* (Dallas: BenBella) 2006, and Michael Greger, *How Not to Die* (New York: Flatiron Books) 2015.

11. Brenda Davis and Vesanto Melina, Davis, *Becoming Vegan: Comprehensive Edition.* (Summertown, TN: Book Publishing Company) 2014.

12. Vesanto Melina, "Redefining Protein Quality: What's New AboutProtein?" https://nutrispeak.com/redefining-protein-quality-whats-new-about-protein/

13. Michael Greger, *How Not to Die,* op. cit.

14. Louie Psihoyos, James Wilkes, James Cameron, Arnold Schwarzenegger, Jackie Chan, Novak Djokovic, et al, *The Game Changers,* September, 2019. https://gamechangersmovie.com/

15. Brenda Davis and Vesanto Molina, *Becoming Vegan* op. cit.

16. USAFacts, "US Obesity Rates Have Tripled Over the Last 60 Years," *USAFacts*, March 21, 2023. https://usafacts.org/articles/obesity-rate-nearly-triples-united-states-over-last-50-years/

17. Ferris Jabr, "Does Thinking Really Hard Burn More Calories?" *Scientific American,* July 18, 2012. https://www.scientificamerican.com/article/thinking-hard-calories/

18. Brenda Davis and Vesanto Molina, op. cit.

19. John A. McDougall, MD and Mary McDougall, *The Starch Solution* (New York: Rodale) 2012, p. 41.

20. Ibid., pp. 41-42.

21. Roland Azar, "75% of Earth Population Are Lactose Intolerant: Here's Why" *Choose Compassion,* September 14, 2017. https://choosecompassion.net/health/75-earth-population-lactose-intolerant-perfectly-natural/

22. Michael Klaper, MD, "Dr. Klaper's Take on Dairy," June 29, 2017. https://www.doctorklaper.com/dairy-free

23. Heather Mclees, "Casein: The Disturbing Connection Between This Dairy Protein and Your Health," *One Green Planet,* May 1, 2023. https://www.onegreenplanet.org/natural-health/casein-dairy-protein-and-your-health/

24. "Why Ditch Dairy? - Health and Performance," *Switch4Good*. https://switch4good.org/health-performance/

25. Wei Zheng, and Sang-Ah Lee, "Well-done Meat Intake, Heterocyclic Amine Exposure, and Cancer Risk," *National Library of Medicine,* January 1, 2010. https://www.ncbi.nlm.nih.gov/pmc/articles/PMC2769029/

26. Janet Stewart, "Researchers Unravel Link Between Herbicide Exposure and Parkinson's," *Parkinson's News Today*, October 27, 2017. https://parkinsonsnewstoday.com/news/technique-explains-herbicide-link-parkinsons-disease/

27. "Aluminum Exposure Again Linked to Alzheimer's Disease," *Neuroscience News and Research,* January 22, 2020. https://www.technologynetworks.com/neuroscience/news/aluminum-exposure-again-linked-to-alzheimers-disease-329670

28. Ramon da Silva Raposo, "Methylmercury Impact on Adult Neurogenesis: Is the Worst Yet to Come from Recent Brazilian Environmental Disasters?" *Frontiers*, November 22, 2020. https://www.frontiersin.org/journals/aging-neuroscience/articles/10.3389/fnagi.2020.591601/full

29. "Ubiquitous Herbicide Glyphosate/Roundup Threatens Nearly All Endangered Species, Says EPA," *Beyond Pesticides,* December 4, 2020. https://beyondpesticides.org/dailynewsblog/2020/12/ubiquitous-herbicide-glyphosate-roundup-threatens-nearly-all-endangered-species-says-epa/

30. Linda Dobberstein, "New Dangers of Glyphosate," *Wellness Resources,* July 25, 2022. https://www.wellnessresources.com/news/new-dangers-of-glyphosate

31. "GE Food and Your Health," *Center for Food Safety,* 2023. https://www.centerforfoodsafety.org/issues/311/ge-foods/ge-food-and-your-health

32. See Stephanie Seneff, *Toxic Legacy: How the Weedkiller Glyphosate Is Destroying Our Health and the Environment* (White River Junction, VT: Chelsea Green, 2021).

33. Joseph Mercola, "Bill Gates' Synthetic Fruit Coating: Even Organic Fruit Is Being Coated with This Stuff," *Truth Comes to Light, May 10, 2023.* https://truthcomestolight.com/bill-gates-synthetic-fruit-coating-even-organic-fruit-is-being-coated-with-this-stuff/

34. For videos of our veganic gardening and Madeleine's food preparation, see www.worldpeacediet.com/cooking-videos/

35. See Vladimir Megré, Leonid Sharashkin, ed., John Woodsworth, tr., *Anastasia* (Ringing Cedars Press, 2005)

36. CSA, an acronym for Community-Supported Agriculture. See https://www.localharvest.org/csa/

37. See T. Colin Campbell, *Whole: Rethinking the Science of Nutrition* (Dallas: BenBella Books, 2014).

38. See John McDougall and Mary McDougall, *The Starch Solution* (Emmaus, PA: Rodale Books, 2013)

39. Alan Goldhamer and Toshia Myers, "An Introduction to the Whole Food, Plant-Based, SOS-Free Diet," *T. Colin Campbell Center for Nutrition Studies,* September 18, 2019. https://nutritionstudies.org/an-introduction-to-the-whole-food-plant-based-sos-free-diet/

40. Unrefined sea salt from ancient sea beds, for example in Utah such as Real Salt, is preferable. Organic miso and tamari are also healthy sources of salt in moderation. https://redmond.life/collections/real-salt

41. This is based on the Macrobiotic principle that animal foods and salt are extremely yang (contractive) and propel us to crave extremely yin (expansive) foods, like sugar, oil, alcohol, tobacco, caffeine, and most drugs, and these then prompt a craving for more yang foods. Vegetables, grains, and legumes are balanced in the middle and should be the mainstay of our diet. See Will Tuttle, *The World Peace Diet*, p. 283.

42. John McDougall and Mary McDougall, *Ibid.*

43. T. Colin Campbell, *The China Study* (Dallas: BenBella Books, 2006)

44. Michael Klaper, "Health Supporting Eating Plan," July 13, 2017. https://www.doctorklaper.com/hsep

45. HealthCraft and SaladMaster are two brands we use, and there may be others. SaladMaster claims to be made from non-recycled metal; though recycling steel is environmentally advantageous, using recycled steel from cars or ships for making cooking pans potentially exposes us to further toxins.

46. See Zendra Palma, MD, "Banned TED Talk: Five Habits for Immune Health," March 20, 2023. https://www.youtube.com/@zandrapalma_md

47. Toshia Myers and Alan Goldhamer, *Can Fasting Save Your Life?* (Summertown, TN: Book Publishing, 2024).

48. See for example, Dr. Michael Klaper, "Fasting – Effective Therapy for Health Concerns," *Dr. Michael Klaper, MD*, January 27, 2017. https://www.doctorklaper.com/fasting

49. Two vegan water fasting facilities are True North Health Center in northern California, and Balance for Life Health & Wellness Retreat in Florida.

50. John C. Umhau and Buddy T., "Why Alcohol is the Most Harmful Drug," *Very Well Mind,* August 29, 2020. https://www.verywellmind.com/alcohol-is-the-most-harmful-drug-3969483

51. See, for example, Masuru Emoto, *The Miracle of Water* (New York: Atria Books, 2011).

52. We have found that the water filters made by Epic and Clearly Filtered are excellent.

53. There are several companies making water structuring devices, Natural Action Technologies being one of them.

54. Lorna Grisby, "Many People Think Cannabis Smoke Is Harmless – A Physician Explains How That Belief Can Put People at Risk," *The Conversation,* August 30, 2023. https://theconversation.com/many-people-think-cannabis-smoke-is-harmless-a-physician-explains-how-that-belief-can-put-people-at-risk-211601

55. Mark Ellison, Forest Bathing: Dr. Qing Li' s Definitive Guide to the Healing Power of Nature," *Hiking Research,* April 16, 2018. https://hikingresearch.wordpress.com/2018/04/16/forest-bathing-dr-qing-li-s-definitive-guide-to-the-healing-power-of-nature/

56. John Whelan, director, *Stink!* Film documentary. 2015. https://www.imdb.com/title/tt4266660/

57. Natalie LaVolpe, "What the Heck Are Soap Nuts?" *Farmers Almanac,* November 10, 2021. https://www.farmersalmanac.com/what-the-heck-are-soap-nuts-24308

58. Thich Nhat Hanh, "The Five Wonderful Precepts," *The Mindfulness Bell,* September 1991. https://www.parallax.org/mindfulnessbell/article/the-five-wonderful-precepts/

Chapter 2—The Second Key: Meditation and Spiritual Practice

59. See, for example, the work of Herbert Benson at Harvard: Carolyn Schatz, "Mindfulness Meditation Improves Connections in the Brain," *Harvard Health Publishing,* April 8, 2011. https://www.health.harvard.edu/blog/mindfulness-meditation-improves-connections-in-the-brain-201104082253

60. Mary Baker Eddy, *Science and Health with Key to the Scriptures*, (Boston: Christian Science Publishing Society, 1923), p. 14.

61. For more information on The Four Viharas and a guided meditation that teaches and aids in practicing The Four Viharas, see http://www.willtuttle.com/viharas.htm

62. For a full discussion of deep veganism, see Chapter Six, "The Benefits of Deep Veganism," in Will Tuttle, *Food for Freedom* (Middletown, CA: 2024), pp. 125-145.

63. Friedrich Miescher Institute for Biomedical Research, "How Neurons That Wire Together Fire Together," *Neuroscience News*, December 23, 2021. https://neurosciencenews.com/wire-fire-neurons-19835/

64. Stephen Covey, *The Seven Habits of Highly Effective People* (New York: Simon & Schuster,1989).

65. Marilia Coutinho, "Are There Benefits to Meditation? 26 Studies Show There Are Many," *Tastylicious,* May 24, 2017. https://tastylicious.com/meditation-benefits-research/

66. Ashley Welch, "How Meditation Can Improve Your Mental Health," *Everyday Health*, August 6, 2022. https://www.everydayhealth.com/meditation/how-meditation-can-improve-your-mental-health/

67. See Dan Brulé, *Just Breathe* (New York: Simon & Schuster) 2017.

68. See Jim Leonard, *Rebirthing: The Science of Enjoying All of Your Life* (San Francisco: Trinity), 1983.

69. See, for example, the website of Fresh and Alive, which makes the "Rest Shield" and the "Home Shield" - https://www.freshandalive.com/

70. See for example this short video of Madeleine ball-dancing: https://www.youtube.com/watch?v=-I-xxdvyV-0

71. See Andrew Holecek, *Dream Yoga: Illuminating Your Life through Lucid Dreaming and the Tibetan Yoga of Sleep* (Boulder: Sounds True), 2016.

72. See this short video for more information: "Power Rest with Madeleine" https://www.youtube.com/watch?v=Xd4nwPGSfp4

Chapter 3—The Third Key: Healthy Relationships and Communication

73. Kyle Benson, "The Magic Relationship Ratio, According to Science," *The Gottman Institute,* https://www.gottman.com/blog/the-magic-relationship-ratio-according-science/

74. Pamela Li, "The Rescuing Hug of Baby Twins Brielle and Kyrie," *Parenting for Brain,* March 19, 2023. https://www.parentingfor-brain.com/the-rescuing-hug-of-baby-twins/

75. Merrell and Lems are, for example, two footwear companies offering thin-soled shoes and sneakers.

Chapter 4—The Fourth Key: The Healing Power of Movement

76. Josh and Rebecca Tickell, *The Earthing Movie: The Remarkable Science of Grounding* (Green Planet Productions, 2018) https://www.earthingmovie.com/

77. Daniel Preiato, "Exercise and the Brain: The Mental Health Benefits of Exercise," *Healthline,* January 31, 2022. https://www.healthline.com/health/depression/exercise

78. For more information, see Exerstrider website: https://www.exerstrider.com/

79. See, for example, Dawn Lester and David Parker, *What Really Makes You Ill? Why Everything You Thought You Knew about Disease Is Wrong* (Independently Published, UK, 2019), and Mark Bailey and Samantha Bailey, *The Final Pandemic: An Antidote to Medical Tyranny* (Independently Published, New Zealand, 2024)

80. Daniel Bubnis, "Everything You Need to Know About the 5 Tibetan Rites," *Healthline,* September 24, 2019. https://www.healthline.com/health/5-tibetan-rites https://www.healthline.com/health/5-tibetan-rites

Chapter 5—The Firth Key: The Healing Power of Nature

81. Association of Nature and Forest Therapy. https://www.natureandforesttherapy.earth/about/the-practice-of-forest-therapy

82. Outward Bound USA: https://www.outwardbound.org/

83. The School of Lost Borders, Big Pine, CA: https://schooloflostborders.org/

84. Geoffrey DeLorme, *Deer Man: Seven Years of Living in the Wild* (London: Greystone, 2022).

85. Susannah Weiss, "5 Pieces of Wisdom from the World's Oldest People," *Bustle,* June 8, 2015. https://www.bustle.com/articles/88712-the-oldest-people-in-the-world-have-many-words-of-wisdom-for-us-so-here-are

Chapter 6—The Sixth Key: The Healing Power of Creativity

86. Elaine Pagels, *The Gnostic Gospels* (New York: Random House), 1969. p. 161. See also Verse 70 of The Gospel of Thomas: http://sites.utoronto.ca/religion/synopsis/gth.htm

87. For information on Dr. Tuttle's original music, see http://willtuttle.com or iTunes, Spotify, Amazon, and other platforms.

88. For more information on our Personalized Music & Art Portraits, see http://willtuttle.com/portraits.htm

89. See Rupert Sheldrake, *A New Science of Life* (London: Blond and Briggs, 1981) and his more recent *The Science Delusion* (London: Coronet, 2012) and *Seven Experiments that Could Change the World* (New York: Riverhead, 1995).

90. David Sorenson, "How Governments use Psychological Manipulation to Change Human Behavior," *Stop World Control*, June, 2022. https://stopworldcontrol.com/behavior/

91. Joseph P. Farrell, "Private Prisons and Corporate (C)Rap "Music," *The Giza Death Star,* November 5, 2018. https://gizadeathstar.com/2018/11/private-prisons-and-corporate-crap-music/

92. Ibid.

93. Joseph P. Farrell, *Microcosm and Medium: The Cosmic Implications of Mind Control Technologies.* (Lulu, 2018.)

94. John Keats, "Ode on a Grecian Urn," 1819. The last lines of this celebrated poem: "Beauty is truth, truth beauty, —that is all Ye know on earth, and all ye need to know."

95. Will Tuttle, *Your Inner Islands: The Keys to Intuitive Living* (Karuna, 2012), p. 54. http://www.worldpeacediet.com/your-inner-islands/

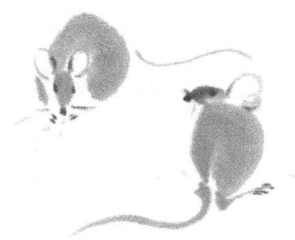